**The Ultimate Guide to**
# SMART
## SHOPPING

Circa 1995, the early days of retail in India, **V. Rajesh** had the interesting challenge of getting women shoppers to accept supermarkets! Since then, his keen understanding of shopper-behaviour has enabled him to devise market-entry strategies as a CXO for many retail giants. The author is now active in the knowledge space and is engaged in sharing his extensive expertise in retail, shopper-marketing and communication through consulting assignments, training programmes and his writing.

Rajesh is also a sought-after speaker and has addressed diverse audiences that range from students to senior corporate professionals on a variety of topics. As a prolific writer, he has written several hundred articles and case studies for leading publications. Rajesh is also the author of the bestseller *Break Free: Unlock the Powerful Communicator in You* published by Rupa Publications in 2016.

His Facebook page is www.facebook.com/retailsme or he can be reached on Twitter @IndianRetailExp.

**The Ultimate Guide to**
# *SMART SHOPPING*

## V. RAJESH

RUPA

Published by
Rupa Publications India Pvt. Ltd 2017
7/16, Ansari Road, Daryaganj
New Delhi 110002

*Sales Centres:*
Allahabad Bengaluru Chennai
Hyderabad Jaipur Kathmandu
Kolkata Mumbai

Text and Illustrations copyright © V. Rajesh 2017
Illustrations credit: Vasudevan Ananthakrishnan

The views and opinions expressed in this book are the author's own and the facts are as reported by him/her which have been verified to the extent possible, and the publishers are not in any way liable for the same.

All rights reserved.
No part of this publication may be reproduced, transmitted, or stored in a retrieval system, in any form or by any means, electronic, mechanical, photocopying, recording or otherwise, without the prior permission of the publisher.

First impression 2017

ISBN: 978-81-291-4861-2

10 9 8 7 6 5 4 3 2 1

The moral right of the author has been asserted.

Printed at Replika Press Pvt. Ltd, India

This book is sold subject to the condition that it shall not, by way of trade or otherwise, be lent, resold, hired out, or otherwise circulated, without the publisher's prior consent, in any form of binding or cover other than that in which it is published.

*Dedicated to Lord Ganesha and Lord Hanuman who guide me in everything I do and inspire me to share whatever I know.*

∞

*Dedicated to all the known and unknown shoppers, my indirect teachers, whose buying behaviour has taught me a lot about this topic.*

# CONTENTS

*Foreword by Shiv Shivakumar, Chairman, PepsiCo India* ix

*Introduction* xv

1. Do Women Really Shop More Than Men? 1
2. Swallow a Chemical Given by Someone You Know! 17
3. I Got the Best Price or Did I? 35
4. The Lady in Red 53
5. FREE is God! 69
6. Pester Power 87
7. I Want It Now! 99
8. Do Shoppers Know How to Get Good Service? 123
9. Becoming a Smart Shopper 149

*Appendix I: Key Takeaway from Each Chapter* 157

*Appendix II: Smart Shopping Habits* 163

*Acknowledgements* 169

# FOREWORD

## *The Smart Shopper and the Marketeer*

Can a consumer be a smart shopper?

If he/she needs to be a smart shopper, then what does the consumer need to know?

These types of questions form the basis of this fourth book by Rajesh, a consumer and shopper expert with enormous practical experience. In a sense, I feel, Rajesh is the Paco Underhill of India with his insights into the average Indian consumer, retailer and shopper.

The Indian retail market valued at $800 billion this year, has been growing at 7 per cent plus for the last seventeen years. India is a large retail market with close to 10 million outlets in fast moving consumer goods, and another 5 million outlets in other industries. The retail landscape is dominated by the traditional 'mom-and-pop' format and the sector employs more than 6 per cent of the Indian workforce.

The Indian consumer has evolved over the years. He/she lived in a shortage situation till the '90s and now has entered a consumer society where real prices in most categories have dropped. Consumers have not had it this good; the range and price value in every category is phenomenal.

There has been a healthy three-way split of value between brands, retailers and consumers. Brands try to maximize margins, retailers try and get more margin from brands and the consumer wants the best value defined as the emotional satisfaction he/she derives from the purchase. This three-way tango can never please all three and hence the science of shopping is essential to create value.

About 42 per cent of consumers live under $1 a day and another 41 per cent live under $2 a day. This means that they are shopping everyday for their daily needs and, in many cases, need the credit facility from the retailer. Many of the projections of Indian retail are based on a big slice of middle-class growth. Growth in middle-class households means a higher demand for durables, cars, and services; not just basic consumer staples.

The development of the food retail chain helps the Indian farmer. Nearly half of India's workforce is employed in agriculture and improvement in consumption of fruits, vegetables and a healthy diet has an all-round benefit.

The Indian retail landscape has undergone dramatic change with the advent of GST. Goods and services are getting transacted with greater transparency and the consumer is moving towards digital payments over time. There is little incentive for retailers and consumers to buy without a bill in the future; in fact there is a lot of disincentive in it GST has taken away the concept of different prices by states on different categories. This is a boon for the shopper.

Rajesh's book focusses on the shopper and what the shopper needs to know to make better decisions. Shopping is never fully a rational exercise and there are deep emotions involved with shopping. Rajesh dwells on ten key themes for better shopper knowledge. Here are the ten gems:

1. The smart shopper is one who is well informed, fully aware of the price-value equation and takes informed decisions. This is truer of an Internet-led, mobile phone-enabled society. Mobile phones and the Internet have helped consumers compare prices and features. However, my experience shows that consumers rarely know price within 5 per cent to 10 per cent of actual price. Consumers do tend to remember round price points and that's why the bulk of the Indian FMCG market is at price points below ₹15 per pack.
2. The Millennial generation has not seen shortage in their lives. They are a different set of shoppers and they can be best described as guilt-free shoppers. This means that they value experiences more than just plain vanilla product solutions.
3. Indian marketers are moving from meeting needs to creating wants and desires. This is very true and forms the inflection point of a consumer society. Penetration is high in most categories and sharp marketers will now focus on driving wants and desires. This will lead to innovation and a higher sensory experience with each product category.
4. Consumers are impacted by all five senses when they shop. The ability to touch, smell, taste, all leads to a higher satisfaction amongst shoppers. A retail outlet that focusses on magnifying the five senses gets better price realization from consumers and is able to drive wants and desires. Car brands charge a premium for some colours, so do mobile phone brands. Some ingredients come at a superior price. Air conditioning in restaurants allows

you to charge a higher price even though the food comes from the same kitchen. Ambience makes a big difference to the shopper.

5. Trust is a basic foundation of transaction between consumer and retailer. Consumers tend to build a shopping habit with an outlet and rarely leave it if their trust is built with every exchange. Trust is more important than truth in a digital world and the good word of public cannot be bought. Retailers will learn how to be smart on the digital medium to earn consumer trust.

6. Indian retail has developed many innovations like New Year's sales, zero margin sales, etc. to get consumers to shop. A lot of these innovations started in Chennai, the first home of organized retail in India, thanks to chains like Higginbotham's, Spencer's, Vivek's, V.G. Panneerdas, Nilgiri's and the coffee chains like Narasu's, Leo, etc. I learnt a lot from each of these chains when I worked as an Area Sales Manager and Regional Manager for Unilever in Chennai.

7. Promotion is an art and picking the right promotion item to offer at the right time is sacrosanct. Rajesh gives us an excellent example of buckets beating gold coins as an offer on a detergent brand. My own experience is that promotions work best on brands in momentum while sales and marketing teams invariably promote a brand or pack when it's in decline or is slowing down. We will see a lot of consumption promotions in the future.

8. Shoppers imagine sales people in retail outlets to have infinite magical properties like guessing the shoe size of a child based on age and height! A knowledgeable sales

person is a delight for a shopper. So, smart sales people must get more product-centric in their stories. I have also seen this in selling mobile phones. A good promoter will draw the consumer attention to email, music and apps in selling a phone, thus exciting the consumer's imagination of his desires. This moves the consumer discussion away from price. In fact, the reason consumers ask the price of something as the first question in an electronics outlet is because the shop promoter has to answer the question. The consumer feels inadequate to talk about electronic features of a product. When the consumer pops the price question, the promoter and the retailer assume that the consumer is price sensitive, which is far from the truth.

9. Pester power or the power of children to influence their parents on their choices is big in India. India has a family size of 4.5, which means there are a minimum of two kids in most households. Understanding the mood of the children in the shopping environment is the smart strategy of a good salesperson. In food and beverage, if a brand does not taste good, it does not go into the home.

10. Consumers in India get surprised by good service. Good service is a huge differentiator for sales. The best in service today tend to be hotels, restaurants, etc. Consistent service needs consistent training on the soft skills. A well-groomed, well-mannered, well-trained person is a diamond in the team.

Rajesh hypothesizes that women are better shoppers than men, and men should learn a few new tricks on shopping.

I enjoyed reading this book and the many nuggets that Rajesh offers based on his real-life examples. This is a great book for anyone interested in consumer and shopper science as a discipline.

> Shiv Shivakumar
> Chairman, PepsiCo India
> 17 July 2017

# INTRODUCTION

In between the various rituals of a typical traditional Indian wedding, there is always a lull. This period seems to be tailor-made for people to catch their breath, rest, recuperate and then jump into the next round of festivities all over again. Needless to say, this is also an excellent opportunity to catch up on gossip, comment on the festivities, etc.

Once a group of people were sitting around during one such lull in a wedding and it was interesting to watch the eclectic mix of people and listen to what everyone was up to. The elderly people (who were in the age group of sixty and above) were commenting about the wedding rituals and how everything is becoming so rushed and commercialized. Their lament was directed to each other and to the few who were relatively young (people who were in their thirties and forties; typically born around 1970s or 1980s who are also referred to as Gen X). These Gen Xers were nodding sympathetically, looking up from their smartphones once in a while. My guess is that they were hoping that the elderly group would give it a rest and let go of the topic. The third group consisted of younger relatives, the children, nieces or nephews of the Gen X group, who had been born after 1990s. They are referred to as Millennials as their birth and growing up years are closer to the turn of the century. I prefer to call them Young Adults and I will explain the rationale as we go along. Now, this last group was also busy with their smartphones and was oblivious to the discussion going on around them.

An elderly gentleman noticed that a part of the audience, the Young Adults, was not even making a pretence of paying attention and decided to do something about it. He loudly remarked that youngsters nowadays have no respect and are constantly glued to their phones. To prove his point, this elderly gentleman called out and demanded to know what the Young Adults were doing with their phones. The first person showed his smartphone's screen and remarked that he was ordering noise-cancelling headphones with extra-bass boosters.

Suddenly, the whole group had a completely new topic to talk about and with widely divergent views and comments.

The elderly person wanted to know why a new headphone was required when the Young Adult already had a pair draped around his neck. He, then, demanded to know the cost of these new headphones and literally fell off his chair to hear that they cost approximately ₹5,000. In all innocence, the Young Adult went on to explain the features of the headphones, asserting the fact that they were wireless. By that point, the Gen X group's attention had been captured and the parents of that Young Adult jumped into the discussion stating that he had purchased the pair he owned now only seven months ago. Therefore, there was no need for new ones.

While the discussion between the parents and the Young Adult went on, the senior citizens jumped into the fray almost as a group and sternly told the Gen X parents that they were at fault. They pointed out how parents 'spoil' their children nowadays by getting them whatever they want and promptly went into a flashback of their own childhood which consisted of scarcity, hardships and all kinds of heart-wrenching scenarios.

The Gen Xers were caught in the middle in more ways than one. They could understand the points of view of both the elderly group and the Young Adults but felt compelled to defend one against the other. They had grown up in households where unnecessary expenses were not allowed and utility was the only rationale behind any purchase. This childhood conditioning was still hidden somewhere in their subconscious. However, the boom in consumer products as well as the increased spending power they enjoyed had changed their orientation to some extent. They could relate to the desire to purchase a new gadget as it was something they also did occasionally. Yet, they were also puzzled by the totally different perspective of their children, the Millennials, when it came to shopping which resulted in many instances of disagreement at their respective homes.

Meanwhile, an elderly gentleman stuck out his hand dramatically and pointed at his watch saying that it was older than the parents of the Young Adults. He proudly proclaimed that the watch was a gift when he graduated and that he had worn it ever since. This declaration prompted a retort from one of the Millennials that the watch being so old was obvious from the old-fashioned dial and style. It now qualifies to be an antique!

Thankfully, at that moment, a waiter served hot snacks and beverages and the topic of shopping, usage of phones, age of the watch, etc. fell by the wayside.

As the larger group broke up, it was interesting to watch each of the smaller groups being puzzled and even resentful about the attitudes of the other groups. While the elderly group could not relate to the waste of money and frequent purchases, the Millennials were aghast that someone could wear the same watch for so many years and tried to figure out what fashion meant to the older generation. On the other hand, the Gen X group was left wondering whose orientation was correct and whether they were indeed spoiling their children by allowing them to spend too much on shopping, especially through the Internet and their smartphones.

This scenario is quite common where varied age groups or different types of shoppers come together and the topic of shopping crops up. Since I have been in the retail sector for more than two decades and have had extensive experience in researching shopper-behaviour, I am often asked about diverse behaviour of shoppers and the reasons for the same. One of the most frequent queries posed to me on several occasions during weddings for example is why do shoppers do what they do? What makes them shop in a particular manner and is there any way to change that? A favourite request is to share tips about how a person can become a better or smarter shopper. Essentially what everyone wants to know is how they can get a better deal or more value out of their shopping.

These questions get addressed to me in the context of my experience related to not only understanding shopping behaviour but also influencing the same. One of my most memorable challenges which also taught me a lot about shoppers' behaviour was related to making Indian housewives accept modern supermarkets in a sustainable and consistent manner. Over the years, I have been a part of senior management of several retail start-ups in India and have had the opportunity of opening various types of stores such as supermarkets, hypermarkets, health and beauty stores, music and entertainment stores, consumer durable and electronic outlets, etc. These varied stores have exposed me to different types of shoppers as well as the same shopper behaving differently when the context of purchase changes. All these rich, interesting and extensive experiences help me when I conduct consulting and specialized training programmes.

The complete experience has been enriching to say the least and I have had several learning moments filled with humour, stress, satisfaction, etc. There have been instances such as, women shoppers saying that they would shop in a nightgown if they felt comfortable in a store, which led to an interesting shopper insight. An occasion when a shopper physically spat at my face is another such learning experience. An agitated elderly gentleman who wanted to beat up a staff member and had to be calmed down, was particularly challenging. A shopper who was willing to tip me just so that I would allow him into the store after it was closed is definitely another great memory. There are so many such experiences that I might pen another volume to just capture those separately. However, I have shared many of these instances in this book as a reference for the reader to help understand the idea and thoughts being discussed.

The idea about a book on this topic actually came to me during a discussion that was somewhat similar to the discussion at a wedding that I have mentioned earlier. It was suggested that if I ever wrote a book on this topic, it would help everyone understand more about shopping and it might help avoid disagreements about it between various types of shoppers. Although, I have written the book, I wonder if disagreements about shopping would ever stop.

Getting back to the scenario of the discussion at the wedding and the conflicting views of various groups, the question remains as to why this difference of opinion and orientation exists at all? The answer to this lies in the paradigm shift that took place in Indian shopping and the resultant shopper-behaviour since the mid-1990s.

In order to understand this transition and the resultant change in mindsets and shopping behaviour, we need to go back in time and start with the '70s.

But, first, let me explain the rationale behind the term Young Adult. I refer to individuals in late teens and early twenties as Young Adults. This group of people is exposed to an overload of information. Also, most of them have their own money to spend. Regardless of whether the money is given to them by their parents or it is earned by them, the spending power exists. Therefore, a lot of their behavioural pattern is like an adult. However, the information they receive and sometimes assimilate is largely second-hand, conceptual and not validated. In addition, the basic physiological aspect of growing-up aligns their behaviour to that of young people. This leads to a contradictory behavioural and thinking pattern where the Millennials often swing between adult, teen as well as childlike behaviours. Hence the term Young Adults.

The '70s in India was a period of measured and planned existence. I use the word existence deliberately as the entire focus of a person in those years was geared towards basic needs. The country was operating with a socialistic mindset and employment opportunities were limited in number as well as scope. The orientation was one of saving for the future instead of spending money today. This was a result of a very poor social security system and limited employment potential. So, people tended to aspire for some kind of permanence concerning jobs, financial means and a basic lifestyle. Saving for a rainy day was the operating maxim and this led to limited spends on discretionary purchases.

Since the joint family system was still around, festival purchases had some comical outcomes. For example, clothes for Diwali would typically mean that the designated elder in the family would purchase metres and metres of cloth and everyone would have shirts stitched from the same. On the festival day, when everyone came out wearing similar shirts, they would all look like members of some musical band.

This saving mindset often went to extreme lengths, literally and figuratively. The half-pants for the boys in the family were often stitched up to their knees. This was to ensure that when they grew taller, new pants would not be needed. Additionally, another inch of cloth was folded and stitched in the hems which would often be opened to make the half-pant suitably longer, just in case! Pants of that length are nowadays called three-fourths or capri pants.

Reuse and recycle were the norms and habits that were engraved into everyone's mind through words and actions. The younger members in the family would invariably end up with the clothes, books, toys, etc. of the older members. To get a new possession was a matter of great pride and joy and was usually reserved for something very special such as a watch for graduation as mentioned by the elderly gentleman. Therefore, the pride in such possessions was immense and lasted for years. Similarly, I am confident that every reader of this book would have at least one elderly relative who, at some point, has mentioned that his pants are ten years old and yet maintained in such good condition.

Shoppers were also constrained by scarce and limited product availability. Waiting for something was the norm and it conditioned the shoppers from that generation to make planned and considered purchases. One had to wait for a few years after booking a scooter and so, when the scooter came, it became a prized possession. This led to a pride in that possession that lasted a lifetime.

I am often asked whether the waiting, the scarcity, the reuse and recycle mindset had all come together to make the shoppers of that generation smarter than their successors. Were they able to get better value for their purchases?

The realistic answer is a yes, as well as a no.

Yes, they might qualify as slightly smarter shoppers mainly because of their functional approach to shopping. Very few of their purchases were impulsive and even those were extremely infrequent. In that context, they were able to manage one of the most important facets which influence shoppers and their shopping behaviour: rational thought versus subconscious impulsive behaviour.

Although, we all like to think of ourselves as rational and logical beings who make their purchase decisions with enough thought behind the same, that is far from the truth. I will discuss this in greater detail in the book and also explain how the current shopping environment actually encourages impulsive behaviour.

The counterpoint is that people from that generation were neither smarter shoppers nor did they get better value out of their purchases. It merely seems so because of the context of their shopping. Their shopping was driven more by availability rather than choice. This meant that they had to end up buying and consuming what was available. Choice in terms of various categories of products, types of products, etc., was extremely limited and was therefore more of a functional transaction. In such a scenario, the shopper being smart or smarter does not arise at all. Even the planned shopping behaviour was because of the economic and socio-economic context. Thus, since this behaviour was thrust upon the generation, one cannot call them smarter shoppers because of that.

This situation started changing in the '90s and India embraced economic liberalization.

The second group in the wedding scenario; the Gen X were typically in their teens or early twenties in the '90s. They were hit by a wave of change in every sphere of their lives.

To start with, the joint-family system had started to fade away.

The choices and decisions of Gen X were being influenced/controlled by their parents, instead of grandparents (or some other elderly relative), who were closer to their age and emotional connect. This enabled a freedom of expression which had not been there in the earlier generations. Although this freedom was limited, it, at least, allowed them to express their wishes, point of view, etc.

The next major influence on this generation came in the form of uncontrolled and free information. This started with the advent of satellite television and then got expanded through the Internet. This proved to be a major social, cultural and economic influence as it suddenly opened a window to the world outside of India.

I still recall the early days of television in India in the late 1970s and early 1980s. Initially, televisions were only black and white, embellished by a screen in front of the original screen. The add-on screen was supposed to protect one's eyes from the harmful effects of watching the television screen. Soon, this add-on screen came with innovations such as the one which magnified the screen. It invariably ended up making the image on the television look terribly bloated and soon fell out of favour. Next, there came one with bands and swathes of colour. This gave the viewer an illusion of watching colour television except in close-up scenes where the actor's face would become multicoloured. The programming choice was limited to good old Doordarshan. It was bad enough that the programmes were terrible even when there was nothing else to compare them with, but, every time any statesman died, an official mourning was declared and one would have to be content with mournful instrumental music for that entire period.

Contrast this with the era of satellite television where there are more channels than what one can see, available twenty-four hours and seven days of the week. The sheer volume of information that was suddenly unleashed on Gen X in the '90s was mind-boggling.

This also coincided with the now historic economic liberalization measures undertaken by the then Prime Minister P.V. Narasimha Rao. The services sector was a new thing and suddenly people were finding new avenues of employment in information technology and business process outsourcing companies. In a span of few years, this enabled people to have more money than what could be spent on their basic necessities or functional requirements. This excess money is referred to as discretionary income because it is usually spent as per the discretion of the person instead of on basic needs by compulsion.

Typically, when economies develop and the population

starts to have discretionary income at their disposal, the first avenue of spending is in the form of eating out. This is what happened in India too. Next is to spend on shopping which is driven by choice and that is usually on lifestyle categories like apparel (clothing). As discretionary income levels go up, people start to spend on consumer durables, automobiles, housing, travel, etc., in that order.

These changes and developments were driven by two simple aspects. The first was the desire for products, etc., which was fuelled by the information boom from satellite television and the Internet. The second catalyst was the availability of money in order to fulfil that desire which was enabled by the boom in economy and increasing levels of discretionary income.

This was also the period when the conditions of scarcity and savings experienced during the growing up years started to conflict with the new-found desire to spend and indulge. Prima facie, this conflict might not seem like a big thing but it was indeed a big influence. It often led to a lot of guilt and post-purchase doubts, which ended up influencing the shopper-behaviour. The parameters used to evaluate a product became complex and confusing and the following story will illustrate this point further.

In 1990s, Maruti cars were the symbol of modern automobiles and were very aspirational. The famous Maruti 800 was coveted and buying one became a kind of milestone for many. It was possibly the first vehicle in India which had a factory-fitted air conditioner. Post 2010, when majority of vehicles have air conditioning by default, this fact might not seem extraordinary. However, in the '90s, when people generally used scooters or motorbikes, it was indeed a big thing.

The major decision for most people while buying the Maruti 800 in the '90s was whether to go for the air-conditioned one or the model without it. The price difference between these two models was significant considering the value of money in those days. Ironically, that was usually not the decision-making parameter when deciding on the AC versus the non-AC version. The key factor was about the mileage as the AC version would run a few kilometres less on a litre of petrol than the non-AC one. This was the main consideration and in light of the relatively low petrol prices then, this seems to be completely irrational. However, that was the shopper mindset—trying to combine aspirational purchases with frugal mentality and that conflict continues in the mindset of Gen X shoppers even today.

The orientation towards air conditioning per se was defined by the perception that AC was an indulgence and only for the rich. This notion was created and reinforced by something as simple as restaurants having separate AC rooms and charging more from patrons choosing to eat in that room. Ironically, this practice continued even into the 2010 and might very well be there for years to come till Gen Xers are alive and willing to pay the differential.

This same behavioural pattern defined the perception of shoppers regarding supermarkets and stores that opened in the mid-90s. On one hand, the aspirational part of the shoppers backed with enough discretionary income would propel them to come to such modern, well-lit, air-conditioned stores; however, they would baulk at making any purchases.

They would have, what I call, the 'AC Maruti' concern which means that anything in an air-conditioned environment was bound to be expensive.

Did such an orientation make them a smarter shopper? Although, I would like to think so, being a part of Gen X, the reality, however, is not so.

They were smarter in a relative context because they were confronted with a high level of choice and complexity in the shopping process. They had to sift through choices of not only products and brands but also various stores and chains that had emerged by then. Their innate sense of caution and saving led them to take more effort in evaluating choices before actually going to any store and making a purchase. This also led to a shift from the age-old custom of buying from a trusted shopkeeper to building trust in a store's brand name and being comfortable shopping in any of the shops of that particular chain.

Conversely, the inherent conflict between spending and saving made them vulnerable to lot of post-purchase doubts and made them respond to discounts and promotional offers in a disproportionate manner. It was mainly due to the rationalization that promotional offers or discounts made the purchase worthwhile and they might not get such a good deal again. The conflict between their growing-up years of scarcity and limited choice again exerted its influence on shoppers in the form of such justification.

The arrival of Millennials changed that to some extent and by the end of the century, acceptance of air conditioning as a part of everyday life started to be seen more often.

That, in a manner of speaking, defined the shopping

orientation and mindset of the Millennial shopper. They were born into and grew up in an environment of availability or maybe even abundance. Shortage and scarcity was not a dominant emotion and more importantly they had access to their own discretionary income from an early age.

It would be incorrect to make a sweeping statement that all Millennials had this mindset and access to discretionary income. Although, this was largely an urban and well-to-do family's orientation, the aspirational part was common across all social classes.

India versus Bharat is a common topic of debate and it details the differences between the urban, educated and well-to-do population as compared to those from the lower economic strata as also from a semi-urban, rural background. Although, there are differences in their orientation and approach to actual shopping, the aspiration part is surprisingly common between these two kinds of shoppers than one would imagine. This is mainly because of common exposure to information in the form of satellite television, Internet, social media, etc. A simple experiment that anyone can undertake to understand this difference as well as the common elements is to watch various channels on television.

There are urban channels which are upmarket and the advertisements for products are in line with high-end shoppers. But, there are other channels which cater to a larger mass market and the products advertised on them are very different. The brands and price points would be different, the benefits promised would be different, etc.

Regardless of these differences, a common thread of aspiration cuts across the shoppers, especially Millennials from both India and Bharat. This fact can be further validated by the reality of purchases made online which is largely driven by Millennials and they cut across geographies and socio-economic classes.

The question of how Millennials are different as shoppers and whether they are the smartest shoppers across these generations comes to mind.

The fundamental difference between Millennials and others is the absence of guilt regarding shopping. It can be traced back to the influences and conditioning during their growing-up years where there was an abundance of available products, enough discretionary income to make purchases, and enough stimuli to trigger a desire for making purchases. They also grew up without understanding the concept of waiting and expect everything to happen instantly. Starting from television programmes to instant noodles, their approach to consumption is immediate and based on instant gratification. Pepsi tapped into this mindset a few years ago through their advertisement which was built around the similar theme of 'Oh yes, abhi'. This line is perhaps the best description of the Millennial shopper. It is one of the reasons why this generation also got labelled as the 'Now Generation'.

This orientation is clearly a strong trigger and driver for online shopping as well as increasing trend of mobile-based apps for shopping. 'Now' being the keyword here. Another dimension is the desire to constantly be current and trendy, which has led to a higher frequency of purchasing than earlier generations.

With Millennials the arrival of the consumption era and consumerism is well established and beyond any doubt.

The question of whether they are the smartest of shoppers across generations again, has a mixed answer of yes and no.

The Millennials, who are younger, have the capability to manage a far higher level of complexity while shopping. This is because their decision-making involves having to evaluate and select from a far larger choice set of products, brands and also places to shop from. This, by itself, qualifies them to be relatively smarter shoppers as they access more information and are better informed than those from previous generations. It is the precise reason why children nowadays define and influence the shopping behaviour of their parents, and this trend will continue even after the Millennials become parents themselves. They would be able to relate to the higher level of information-seeking and -processing abilities that their children would have and, therefore, would be open to consultative shopping patterns.

However, on the other hand, there is an element of instant gratification which exerts a strong unconscious pressure to complete the shopping transaction. It would invariably make them vulnerable to decisions which are not well thought-out and rational. In that context, they might not qualify to be smart shoppers at all.

It is time to define this term 'smart shopper' as I have used it and also make observations about being one or not. For me, a smart shopper is essentially someone who clearly understands what he wants, evaluates all the options available, and then makes an informed and rational choice before the actual shopping transaction begins. This could be a drawn-out and detailed process in the context of high-value products or for those products where the consumer has a high emotional involvement. Alternatively, it could be a short and maybe a split-second action for certain other product categories.

For example, a mother would invest considerable time and effort when choosing products for her newborn or child. However, she might not invest the same kind of time and effort once the child has grown beyond a particular age.

The reality, which might be shocking to most of the readers, is that majority are NOT smart shoppers and hence, there was a need for a book on this topic.

Over the years of observing and understanding shopping behaviour, I have seen a common thread that is, although there are elements of some rational thought and logic behind the decision-making process, shopping still largely remains an impulsive, subconscious activity. This is a fact which cuts across gender, age and even cultural differences.

At a broad level, shopping appears to be a simple and straightforward activity. The process starts when a person perceives a need which requires fulfilment. By definition, needs are very basic in nature. One of the most enduring and detailed explanations on this topic is a psychological theory on the hierarchy of needs by Abraham Maslow. It was part of a paper written by him in 1943 titled, 'A Theory of Human Motivation' which is worth exploring if anyone wants to delve deeper into this topic.

Once a person perceives a need, they start to explore ways to fulfil that need and that is referred to as 'wants'. In simple terms, wants are the preferred options to fulfil a need. A very basic example pertains to thirst or hunger. When a person feels thirsty, that is a need. That person might want water, soft drink, juice or any other option to fulfil that need. The wants are influenced by a variety of factors including the financial means of that person. It defines their search for options which would satisfy their need.

This is an important element when understanding shopper-behaviour. This shift from needs dominating the shopping decision to wants becoming a bigger influence is significant. When the shopper focuses on needs, the decision-making process is far more functional in nature. Comparatively, when the focus shifts to wants, it becomes more aspirational. This shift goes back to what I had mentioned earlier regarding increased levels of exposure as well as more money in the wallet. The online order of headphones by Millennials is a classic example of a focus on wants instead of needs.

The next step in the shopping process is to search for information about options. Today, this is a multifaceted process as compared to earlier because of multiplicity of information sources as well as increase in shopping choices, both in terms of products and stores.

Nowadays, searching for information is far easier, thanks to the Internet. It has led to shoppers doing their searching on multiple levels. The starting point is to search for product and brand options. This experience has evolved to such an extent that a shopper can experience every aspect of a product except handling it physically.

Recently, I wanted to get a backpack for my travels and was quite specific in terms of the features that I wanted it to have. After having shortlisted a few bags, I was able to check out details of the bags in every facet possible including seeing videos online which showed the bags' various features along with other users' feedback and comments. This helped me finalize the product and brand without having to step out of my home. This was something I could not have imagined just a decade ago. The next part of the search is concerned with where to purchase the product from. Price and promotional offers do play a dominant role in this search. However, the interesting reality is that in many instances the shopper ends up making the final choice based on completely different parameters. In many cases, the decision about the product and the brand also undergoes a paradigm change because of external influences and stimuli.

The search phase of the shopping process is largely rational and logical. However, when shoppers are confronted with new options and choices that they had not considered before, the subconscious, impulsive behaviour kicks in and ends up influencing the actual shopping. This is also because of the fact that there are many categories where the focus on wants ends up short-circuiting the search part. In such cases, shoppers jump straight into the purchase. This behaviour is becoming more frequent due to a variety of factors.

The next few steps in shopping involve actual shopping, using the product and being influenced about the next purchase. The actual shopping experience plays a huge role in the entire process mainly because retailers have understood that it is open to influence since it is done on a subconscious level and is also impulsive.

It would be an understatement to say that shopping today is a complex mix of rational inputs and thoughts along with various subtle, emotional and sensory stimuli that trigger strong subconscious, impulsive responses. These impulsive responses tend to override the rational part of shopping in most cases and constrain a person from being a truly smart shopper simply because their reaction to stimuli ends up being exactly the intended response.

This book will detail, decode and explain the various facets which influence a shopper as well as share the secrets that retailers use to trigger emotional responses.

One such parameter is the type of shopper a person happens to be as that influences how they process various stimuli. Till now, we have explored the generational influence on shoppers and their behaviour. However, that is not the only dimension, and this book will explain various other types of shoppers in terms of gender, cultural orientation, etc. The various emotional aspects that influence a shopper, independent of the retailer's stimuli, will also be discussed in the forthcoming chapters because they play a significant role and knowing about them is another facet of becoming a smart shopper.

For example, the role of any shopper's level of trust in the entire shopping process is very crucial. It plays a big role in how we process the information being received and the extent to which we are ready to believe the same. It might appear to be a rational or logical thing but, in reality, it is far more biased and driven by our subconscious conditioning and thinking.

Lastly, I would like to share some more background about this book and what you can expect from the forthcoming chapters.

I have already mentioned about my extensive experience in retail and my understanding of shopper-behaviour which enable me to share such detailed insights about shopping. In this book, I would be attempting to answer the basic question which is posed to me very frequently: how can a person become a smart shopper?

In the context of the onslaught of advertisements and the availability of varied retail venues for shoppers, this question is very relevant as everyone wants to get the best deal and believe that they are smart shoppers. Easy credit in the form of multiple credit cards has only made this a bigger concern as many people look with dismay at their credit card statements and often wonder why they ended up purchasing so many things and spending so much.

The book will outline various types of shoppers and kinds of shopping behaviours which might strike a chord with you and help you identify the kind of shopper you are. Going forward, the book will detail various cues, triggers and influences that play on your conscious and unconscious mind. Lastly, the book will have a broad and simplified overview of some of the conceptual theories which marketers and retailers use to understand and influence shoppers.

The intent behind writing this book is to make the reader aware of what typically happens in their minds, both at a conscious and an unconscious level during the shopping process. It might also help you to understand some of the 'whys' behind the shopping being done by you and that could help you manage your shopping in a better manner.

The book is set in the Indian context as you would have understood from the Introduction. However, the details mentioned in various chapters are global in nature as many aspects of the shopper-behaviour are common. This is especially true of the various emotional and impulsive triggers and the resultant responses. It is also a fact that Indian shoppers are evolving and maturing as fast, if not faster, as their global counterparts, and in that context, the factors impacting Indian shoppers are also global in nature. There are many stories, anecdotes and examples in the book to explain various points. These are about people with varied backgrounds, ethnicity, age, gender, etc. Every such example is only intended to explain the related point and there is no disrespect meant to that respective group of shoppers. I do hope that the reader does not take any offence to any of these stories and examples.

Shopping behaviour changes and is dynamic by nature. A classic example is the evolving shopper-behaviour with regard to online shopping in India. I have tried my best to keep this book as contemporary as possible and hope that, as a reader, you would be able to relate to everything in the book, irrespective of when you read it.

Shopper- and consumer-behaviour is a vast subject which has multiple complexities because of the interplay of various conscious and unconscious influences. The impact of external stimuli and the resultant variable responses only increase this complexity. I have attempted to present it in a simplified and easy-to-understand manner and hope that this will be helpful to every reader.

Last, but not the least, is a small challenge for the reader.

I am fairly confident that in spite of reading the book and understanding the various points, there is a very high probability that you will continue to be influenced by your emotional, unconscious, impulsive decisions instead of the rational thought processes. This statement leads to the question about the very purpose of this book and why you should read it. There are two reasons which I can give you for the same.

Firstly, the book will make you aware of why and how your shopping is done. Although, you might find it difficult to change overnight, this awareness might slowly bring a higher understanding and some more rational logic into your shopping decisions.

Secondly, you might be able to recognize some of these influences and even if you succumb to them, you will at least know about the same.

Retailers can understand the influences on shopper-behaviour and use many of the elements mentioned in the book to improve their stores as well as shoppers' satisfaction level. Needless to say, a good understanding of the various factors that influence a shopper and acting on them will help in increased sales.

Despite my statement about shoppers not being able to change, there will be some people who will be able to internalize the contents of this book and actually evolve into smart shoppers by bringing in a higher level of rational and logical thought into their shopping. It would be fantastic if many of you are able to do this and I would be delighted to hear about your stories of becoming smart shoppers.

I request all of you to post your experiences as shoppers as well as how you were able to morph into smart shoppers on the Facebook page of this book titled 'SMART Shopping' (search for @SMARTShoppingbook). I would be glad to read your experiences and I am sure there will be many more people out there who could learn from your stories and be motivated by them.

Now, it is full speed ahead to becoming a Smart Shopper.

# 1

# DO WOMEN REALLY SHOP MORE THAN MEN?

*Types of shopper-behaviour*

Do women really shop more than men? Are they compulsive window shoppers and take forever to make purchases? Do young adults and teenagers shop more and tend to splurge? Are men really very bad at shopping?

These are the questions which come to mind when one keeps on hearing clichés and jokes regarding shopping. In fact, if one were to do an online search about men and women shopping, the results would have various images which would be similar to the following drawing.

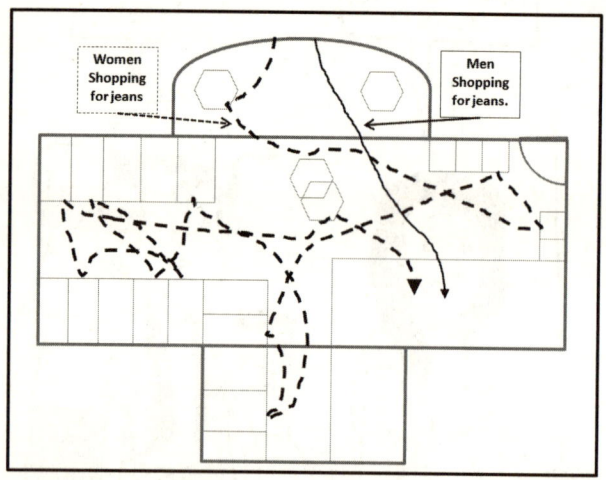

Then, the question arises whether there is some truth in the above-mentioned questions and why it happens if it is true?

Yes, there is an element of truth in the statements mentioned above. The shopping orientation and behaviour of men and women are very different. Even the changing behaviour of the modern or metrosexual men is different from that of women. The rationale for this difference is supposedly linked to the evolutionary start when all of us were still living in caves and were following the traditional roles of men and women.

Men were hunters and they became conditioned to follow a focused and task-oriented approach in this role. After all, a hunter cannot stop to smell the flowers and appreciate the natural beauty around him. Few men who would have done that might have ended up as the prey. In that process, men's orientation for a successful hunt and maybe even survival became linked to a single-point agenda without any distractions.

This also influenced their physical characteristics such as eyesight. Men tend to look at and focus on few things in their field of vision, which itself is narrower than that of most women. Another aspect of male behaviour is to have minimal and functional communication. This is something I have written about extensively in my earlier book called *Break Free: Unlock the Powerful Communicator in You* where I have explained why and how communication issues crop up between men and women, as well as what should be done to avoid the same.

The traditional women's role was linked to the cave, gathering food, managing the chores, etc. This required them to be able to handle numerous tasks and activities at the same time while also being physically alert to multiple sensory influences. A typical day might have consisted of having to handle an open fire, taking care of children who might be playing nearby by gathering and preparing food while also being alert for any animals approaching as well as any other threat.

This led them to be more adept at multitasking as well

as receiving and processing multiple sensory responses simultaneously. For example, a woman can drive while listening to her children recount what happened at school, listen to music and yet be able to think and plan some important work that needs to be done. Most men, including myself, would prefer others in the car to be quiet, especially when the traffic is bad, as one needs to concentrate while driving.

Women have a wider range of vision compared to men and that is a fact; their peripheral vision is better and wider than that of men. This could very well be the reason why mothers are supposed to have eyes on the back of their heads and can catch their children if they are up to any mischief.

Another important difference between men and women is regarding their interactions and communications. Men approach communication from a functional and linear perspective. This means that they prefer to speak less and many a times it makes them sound abrupt to the point of being rude. Small talk, which is communicating only for the sake of establishing a social rapport, is something that most men are not comfortable with and when anyone indulges in small talk, they become impatient. Women, on the other hand, like to connect and any interaction is an opportunity to do so. My book, *Break Free: Unlock the Powerful Communicator in You* has more details on this topic and might be worth a read.

The question is how do all these differences influence the shopping behaviour of a male versus a female shopper?

Let me explain this using the earlier diagram as a reference.

When a male shopper goes into a mall to purchase a pair of jeans, he is rarely thinking about anything else. He goes in seeking the jeans in the same manner as a hunter stalks his prey. He goes in, locates the jeans, purchases them and is out as fast as possible. Since his attention as well as his vision is focused on locating the store and, then, the jeans, they rarely register anything else. Men are almost like horses with their blinkers on. They see one thing and have only one thought. Buy jeans!

On the other hand, when a woman goes shopping she is not only open to multiple sensory influences including a wider range of vision but she also has a to-do list running in the back of her mind. Her ability to be receptive to various stimuli makes her aware of as well as explore far more options. So, the woman's path in the diagram not only includes the purchase of jeans but also involves purchasing accessories or something for her children, spouse, etc. She might even remember that a gift had to be purchased, which gets done and struck off her to-do list. So, prima facie, it might appear that a woman spends more time on shopping, but, the reality is that she ends up finishing multiple chores at one shot.

Similar to the cliché about women shopping more is the statement about men always forgetting to buy some of the things they were supposed to purchase. This is the result of their single-point focus, the jeans-only orientation. Needless to say, if there are multiple things that are supposed to be purchased, a woman shopper would be better compared to a man who even has a list in his hand.

Retailers are aware of this knowledge and make the best use of it. Stores and categories which cater mainly to men are usually displayed in a simple, easy-to-see and -access manner. There are minimalistic sensory influences and distractions. On the other hand, stores which cater predominantly to women are far more colourful, have multiple displays, higher levels of engagement through every possible sensory element including personal interaction. Next time you visit a clothing store, compare the mannequin display in the men's section with the one in the women's section. The women's mannequin will have a higher level of display and will include accessories and additional items like bags because they will be more receptive to such multiple influences.

Both these approaches have their own advantages and disadvantages. The men's orientation is good enough for functional shopping while it might be a handicap for lifestyle shopping. The reverse is true for women.

As mentioned earlier, levels of communication and interaction preferred by men and women are completely different. It has a huge implication on the service provided by the retail staff as well as the training given to them. The best example for this differentiated service is to observe the way a salesman interacts with ladies in a sari shop. They would have casual conversations, ask questions and communicate to connect with customers. I know many men who get impatient and irritated by these talks and sometimes even snap at the salesman to get on with displaying the saris. Such men do not realize that this interaction is as important to the women shoppers as making the purchase itself. It is an integral part of shopping.

Women would love to shop with their spouse or partner but they do not enjoy it for the basic reason that their orientation is very different. While women want to interact and explore various options and choices, men want to complete the transaction and leave. If not as a smart shopper, a smart spouse or a smart partner would understand this fundamental difference and change their orientation towards shopping for each other.

The desire for interaction is equally important and can be illustrated by the following example. There is a story about an Indian woman who goes to the United States to visit her daughter's family. She takes it upon herself to do the frequent vegetable shopping since she is staying with them. On her first shopping expedition, she is seen bargaining with the shopkeeper. This was an awkward scenario as such behaviour is usually not an accepted practice in the USA. When the son-in-law hears about this, he decides to resolve the issue by neither hurting the old woman's feelings nor alienating the neighbourhood store owner. He figures out an ideal solution wherein he approaches the shopkeeper and requests him to bargain but allow the woman some discount. Then, once a week, the son-in-law would go to the store and pay the difference that the shopkeeper had given as a discount to the woman. In the end, everyone was happy.

The woman might have been bargaining not only to get a better price but also for an opportunity to interact. It would have been quite possible that a man would not have done this as interaction is not a priority in their shopping process. It is no wonder that men are not very good when it comes to bargaining with shopkeepers. The importance of bargaining and getting a good price in this story is an example of the generational impact on shopping which is also next on the agenda.

In the later part of 2015, I was travelling to Bengaluru by the Shatabdi Express and a gentleman in the seat behind me was having such a loud and animated conversation on his phone that it was hard not to hear his side of the phone call. The gist of his conversation was an extreme displeasure about an online purchase made by the person on the other side of the call. It appeared to be his son who seemed to have ordered something from an online shopping site which was the trigger for this gentleman's angst. He went on to declare how this was a colossal mistake because they might end up getting a faulty product as a best-case scenario or maybe even a brick instead of the product in the worst case. He went on to vehemently denounce all online shopping sites as cheats and vented his anger on the person on the other end of the call by predicting all the possible things that could go wrong.

This is a clear case of the mindset and orientation defining the response to a situation, namely shopping. The growing up condition of the father seems to be influenced by caution and a sense of unease with regard to transactions which do not have a physical feel to it. This could be the influence of experiences during his formative years where shopping was a physical activity done from a physical person. The relationship with that person gave the shopper confidence with regard to the transaction and reassured him that the shopkeeper would help him in case of any issue. The experience would also have included the absence of formal customer service platform for any of the products purchased which only reinforced the dependence and, therefore, trust in the shopkeeper.

The conversation I overheard is a classic conflict happening between the Gen X shopper versus a Millennial, especially in India. This incident reminded me of my own experience in the '90s when I informed my family that I would be joining a start-up venture which planned to open supermarkets in India under the brand name of Foodworld. Almost every elder in the family denounced this decision as foolhardy and proclaimed that I was committing professional hara-kiri. These comments were laced with indignation as to who would want to shop at these new air-conditioned stores which were clearly more expensive as compared to the good old trustworthy neighbourhood grocery stores.

These differences are linked to our conscious as well as subconscious conditioning which starts from our childhood itself. Behavioural studies show that a person's mind gets bombarded with cues right from their birth and these influence their attitude, personality, outlook, etc. It is said that the mindset of a person is defined by the time they are five years of age and that ends up dictating his behaviour and choices in life. Obviously the environment in those formative years has a strong role to play in defining one's shopping behaviour.

Age is a very important factor that determines perception, priorities and behaviour. At different stages of a person's life, his priorities change and define his choices. For example, a young adult starting his first job is usually carefree and his attitude is oriented more towards lifestyle choices instead of functional ones. Spending money on shopping and entertainment is easy and frequently done. Even young adults, who need to financially support their families, tend to use their share of income for lifestyle expenditure. The same person's orientation starts to change over the years when financial demands of his own family in terms of spouse and children become a part of his life. Regardless of this change, certain fundamental shopping patterns don't change for a person belonging to a particular generation. For example, an elderly person who is financially well-off might still be frugal about spending and his shopping would accordingly be very functional even though he can afford to spend more.

However, this behavioural patter is not static. It changes based on the period of one's birth and exposure during the growing up years. This is referred to as generational influence and pertains to the conditioning the person gets during their formative years. The anecdote about the discussion during a wedding amongst three distinct age groups earlier in the book is an example of generational influence which creates differing points of view and perceptions.

As a shopper, this aspect is very important since generational influence tends to define their shopping behaviour in terms of choice of outlets, products, brands, etc. The most dramatic shift, in the Indian context, is centred around three distinct events: the shortage and uncertainties of '70s and '80s, the economic liberalization of '90s and the advent of technology in the later years. When faced with a similar scenario, a person from each of these time periods would react very differently and that is usually a subconscious response.

One fundamental reality which influences shopping is the availability of money or the financial situation of the shopper. Interestingly, this was an important influence years ago and is becoming far less of a differentiator nowadays. The younger generation shoppers across the various socio-economic levels are tending to behave in a similar manner. The best example for this is with regard to smartphone purchases. The average period of ownership before a person buys another phone could be less than a year. This buying pattern is common amongst the younger shoppers and the only differentiation is whether they buy a leading top-end brand or an economical one. At the very least, they would buy a second-hand phone but definitely do so once a year.

As the differences between genders have pros and cons for the respective shopper, the generational influence also has the same.

The Gen X shopper is far more planned and cautious in their shopping as compared to the Millennial shopper. Therefore, Millennials would be far more likely to purchase new products, new models, etc., as compared to a Gen X shopper. This different orientation also defines the concept of value for these two types of shoppers. Gen X and older generations place importance on the functional aspects, durability, etc., and that is an important component of value for them. Whereas, Millennials place a premium on latest features and trends. This is also because they replace the products more frequently and hence shop more often.

The older generation or Gen X's approach of prudence and caution is definitely of value especially when purchasing products that cost more. On the other hand, Millennial's approach might help in purchasing lifestyle products.

Varied shopping behaviour is not limited to the influence of gender and age alone. Cultural context and the category of products being purchased also play a significant role in the way people shop.

For example, a person who is a tea drinker would be indifferent to purchasing coffee for someone else. The very habit of drinking tea is linked to one's growing up years and the resultant conditioning. This habit is usually linked to places and local cultural practices. In Tibet, there is a local brew called Po Cha which is also referred to as butter tea. It is made from tea, salt, butter and ends up tasting more like a soup. A shopper with this growing-up orientation and conditioning would approach the purchase of tea from a very different perspective than say a shopper who hails from Assam or any other regular tea-consuming region. The basic product is same and yet the shopper-behaviour and response varies because of one's cultural orientation.

During a store opening, I was amazed to see customers whipping out their mobile phones at the billing counter to recalculate the entire bill, especially the discounts and promotional offers, just in case the computer had been wrong! This kind of shopper-behaviour would not be seen in any other region, state or country largely because of the different cultural influences.

One amusing incident during another store opening involved a well-to-do woman bargaining for an additional free plastic bucket and then driving away in a Mercedes Benz satisfied that she had two buckets instead of one. The irony was that the cost of those buckets would not even cover the cost of fuel for such a car! After so many years, I still wonder if that woman would have created such a fuss in a lifestyle store as compared to a supermarket. This is an interesting confluence of the impact of gender, category of products being purchased, as well as the generational impact. I doubt if the same would have happened if even one of these influences had been different.

These three examples would illustrate how the shopping behaviour and orientation change based on cultural context as well as the category of products being purchased. This is again linked to our conscious and subconscious conditioning which manifests itself as shopping behaviour.

It is the combination of all these influences which makes a person indulge in shopping and other related activities. One such common activity is window shopping. It refers to seeing various products available for sale and checking out the prices, designs, features, etc. Contrary to common perception, window shopping is indulged in by every kind of shopper. Men, women, young, old—everyone does window shopping. It varies only by the degree to which this is done and how it is done. For example, many men read up about gadgets and see videos about the same online. This is the same as a woman checking out mannequins in an apparel store's display.

Now, the question is whether one of these influencers is the dominant one and does it override all the other aspects?

Yes, the gender influence does dominate and it might be because of centuries of conditioning. Its dominance might also change over a period of time. The impact of generational influence and cultural parameters come next, and lastly is the context of shopping with regard to the category of products being purchased.

In the many years of my retail journey, I have opened stores of various sizes, in different cities that offer a varied range of products. The one thing which has been a constant source of learning, as well as amazement, has been the widely different shopper-behaviours I have seen over the years. This is because each one of us has a distinctly unique shopping behaviour. This distinction comes into play because of the multiplicity of influences on our shopping such as gender, age, the category of products being purchased, etc. It is no wonder that the sale of gift cards and coupons is increasing, especially in India. It is easier to give money in the diplomatic form of a gift card when shopping behaviours are so very divergent.

Although, each one of us have our own unique shopping behaviour, the broad influences discussed till now might help you decipher your shopping behaviour and maybe modify it if you feel it is worth doing so.

## KEY TAKEAWAY

> Shopping behaviour varies based on gender, age and the category of product being purchased.
> Men are more functional in their shopping approach while women might actually be better shoppers.
> Women might shop for a longer period but also finish more chores during that time.
> The older generation and Gen X are more functional and value-driven.
> Millennials' priority while shopping is about latest trends and new features.

## SMART SHOPPING HABITS

> Men should always shop with a list. Chances of missing out things would be less.
> Women can verbalize the to-do list in their minds when shopping with a male as this would avoid misunderstandings.
> When shopping for a woman, focus on the sensory aspect and appeal. The reverse should be done when shopping for men; focus more on the functional and utility aspects in that case.
> When shopping with or for Millennials, focus on the latest, trendy categories. Millennials who are shopping for their parents should keep in mind that their parents have a different orientation and might not appreciate the same thing.

> Avoid being judgemental about different shopping orientations. Each is an outcome of certain influences and has its own advantages.

# 2

## SWALLOW A CHEMICAL GIVEN BY SOMEONE YOU KNOW!

*I trust; therefore I buy!*

Imagine that you have known me for a few years. It is not as if we are close friends or bosom pals; more like acquaintances who know each other by sight.

Now, suppose that I offered you a whitish substance and suggested that you swallow the same. My contention would be that it is good for you and you will benefit from swallowing this substance. How will you react?

The chances are that many of you would be shocked by this suggestion and wonder how I could even think of suggesting something like this. Some of you might be curious to find out about the substance and might get the name of that substance from me which would be completely alien and make no sense at all. A small minority, who are adventurous enough, might even risk swallowing it.

Remember that I am a mere acquaintance who has offered this substance to you. Although, the mere suggestion might be quite shocking and not even worth considering, the reality is that a majority of shoppers in India do just the same quite frequently. It is quite possible that you have also done this, at least a few times in your life.

Are you shocked?

Let me explain and point out the obvious.

In the case of minor ailments or at least what one would consider as minor, a person tends to approach their regular medical shop and ask for some medicine for the same. This could be for a headache, a stomach upset, or even a fever. The person in the medical shop, whom you know by sight and might not even know by name, would suggest some medicine. The chances are that you will be willing to purchase what was suggested and take that medicine. In absolute terms, you would have done exactly what I was suggesting—that is, taking some chemical substance from an acquaintance.

Why is it that you might hesitate to do so if I offered you this medicine but are willing to do the exact same thing if suggested by the medical shop person? The irony is that you do not know if the person working in the shop is even qualified to suggest medication. Yet, majority of shoppers are fine to buy and take the suggested medicine.

There are various theories and concepts that can explain this behavioural pattern. In simple terms, this behaviour is a direct outcome of your trust in the shopkeeper.

Trust is a powerful emotion and motivation. The power of trust extends across many facets of our lives such as religion and some of our basic beliefs as well as values. On a side note, trust is also the key force that drives massive enterprises across the world of religion and God-men/women.

Trust and faith are two very powerful forces, although belief in them is based on an individual's perception which differs from person to person. The power of faith and the impact of prayers are topics of ongoing scientific debates. Over the years, several studies have tried to prove whether prayers make a difference to a patient's health and recovery. Nevertheless, there has been no statistically validated support for this. However, I can confidently say that trust does have a large role to play in shopping behaviour.

Let me share an anecdote from the early '90s to illustrate how trust defines shopping behaviour after which I will explain the workings of our mind in this regard.

During the early days of supermarkets, our team did a quick dipstick study in a Chennai locality to find out why shoppers were coming to the store but were not purchasing any groceries. Grocery purchase, especially rice or wheat (atta), is a very important representation of trust in the Indian context. The exercise involved collecting rice samples from households and in return giving a sample of that rice which was sold in our supermarket.

The rice samples that were collected were individually cooked to evaluate their quality. Then, they were compared with the quality and price that was offered in our supermarket chain. It was quite surprising to note that the majority of samples were at least a grade lower than what was being sold at our stores. Ironically, this lower grade rice was being purchased at prices which were higher compared to our supermarket.

The same customers were contacted again to get their feedback about the rice samples that had been given to them. Most of them said that the rice quality was very good and they were happy with them. These shoppers were then told about the price at our supermarket as compared to the price they were paying right now.

Their reactions are an enduring testimony to the role of trust in shopping. The reactions ranged from mild to severe denial to disbelief. They stated confidently that although the rice sample we had given was good, the rice that they usually purchased was better. The fact remains that they were not ready to look at their purchases in an objective and rational manner.

Whenever a shopper survey is done and people are asked about the reasons why they frequent a particular store, the responses have broadly been the same since early 1990s. The responses would list quality, prices and the range of products available as the most important expectations. This would be followed by convenience and service. Relationship might find a place at last, almost as an afterthought.

The irony is that shoppers trust an outlet based on their relationship. Hence, they believe that they are getting the best deal in terms of the other parameters which consist of quality, price, etc. This is clearly a perception and proves the maxim that perception is reality. What you perceive becomes the reality you believe in.

This interesting dynamic in shopper-behaviour is because of the generational influence on shoppers. Earlier generations and even a majority of Gen X shoppers have been largely anchored to the same city, locality and even house. This led them to develop long-term relationships with neighbouring stores which still continues to dominate their shopping preferences. On the other hand, few of the Gen Xers and many Millennials have been mobile with regard to their job and place of residence. Thus, they do not have similar deep-rooted trust and relationships with stores. However, even in their case the aspect of trust plays a crucial role but in a slightly different manner. They have learnt to trust a retailer based on not only individual experiences but also collective feedback. Since they are far more active on social media platforms, the collective experiences from their circle of contacts does influence their trust levels.

Regardless of generational or gender influence, the creation of trust is directly linked to their expectations being met. The key expectations of any retail customer start from basic functional expectations and peak with relationship-based needs and requirements.

## Basic Expectations–

When a person goes into a shop to purchase something, his fundamental expectation obviously deals with the products that are being sold at that store. Any customer's basic expectation from a store is availability, quality, price, hygiene, convenience and service. Usually when these are met, the customer does not think too highly of a store and does not talk about it. After all no one will sing praises if the cups and saucers in a restaurant are clean. However, if any of the above-mentioned elements are not met, the customer is very vocal about it and spreads the negative word of mouth to all and sundry.

## Emotional Expectations–

Once the customer buys what he/she intended to purchase and is satisfied with the basics like price and quality, he starts to expect more. The customer expects that the retailer is responsive. Responsiveness can be manifested in the form of having the right products that a customer is seeking or taking the trouble to procure the same. The ultimate manifestation of being responsive is to be able to anticipate and cater to the customer's needs and expectations be it for products or services. It is this responsiveness that actually creates credibility in the shopper's mind and leads to trust. The extent to which a shopper trusts the retailer varies, and the highest form of trust is when they will follow the retailer's suggestion without question. This is the rationale behind why you might take a medicine suggested by your medical shop person without any question.

The conscious or overt expectations of shoppers have not changed much and continue to be linked to products in terms of their availability, quality, range, price, etc. The secondary level of conscious expectations is with regard to the softer aspects like convenience, service, etc. Both are obviously influenced by various aspects that have been mentioned in the first chapter such as age, gender, socio-economic background, etc. If the retailer or service provider meets or exceeds these expectations, then the shopper starts to believe in him. The level of trust keeps on increasing with each such experience of expectations being managed positively till a point where the trust ends up defining the expectation.

A relevant example is low-cost airlines in India. The first such operator was Deccan Airlines which started off in the early part of this century. The stated objective of the promoter was to attract first-time fliers as an option instead of them being an alternative to existing frequent fliers. However, two classes of fliers ended up using this airline. One was the stated target group of people who found the fares very attractive and wanted to experience flying. The other group was of frequent fliers who ironically opted for this airline when booking tickets for their personal travel. This is also an example of how the same shopper/consumer behaves differently based on the context of consumption.

Getting back to the topic of expectations, these two groups ended up having very different expectations. The first-time fliers were awed by the experience and were perfectly happy to wait for delayed flights, low level of service, etc. Their benchmark was the other modes of travel that they had been using. On the other hand, the regular fliers were obviously disappointed since they were comparing the experience with the other airlines. Ironically, the fact that they were paying a fraction of the cost as the ticket price completely vanished from their conscious thought. This led to a lot of dissatisfied customers who were vociferous about their being unhappy. It ended up creating a poor image for the airline as a whole. It is important to note that I am not commenting here on the business aspect which led to the sale of this airline as it is a completely different topic.

Fast forward to 2005–6 and more low-cost airlines came into the Indian skies and they have been around since. The expectations from these low-cost airlines have had a paradigm shift even in the minds of regular fliers. The key expectation of passengers now is that the flight leaves on time. All the other expectations have either become watered-down or have simply vanished. For example, the availability of free food as a given is no longer true. The expectation is not there and so if any airline does not offer food in the flight, it is considered acceptable.

So, trust is built on the experiences of how the shopper expectations were managed. In case of positive outcomes, the shopper starts to trust the shop and the staff or owner/manager.

The second aspect which drives trust is equally powerful and acts on a subconscious level.

This aspect of trust is driven by the fact that majority of customers do not know how to evaluate the quality of the product they usually purchase. Their faith and trust on the product's brand or the store or both makes the shopper believe that they are making the right purchasing decision. Although, many shoppers pride themselves on being well-informed and, therefore, believe that they are making the right choice, this is often a perception.

Millennials belong to that shopper group which truly believes that they do enough research and make informed decisions. But, they usually end up trusting the brand, store, or in most cases, their influential group of peers as well as opinionated leaders.

Let me illustrate this with an example with regard to mobile phone purchases.

As mentioned, Millennials change their mobile phones far more frequently as compared to Gen X shoppers. If one was to ask any of the Millennials to list out the rational reasons for this frequent change, they might list the following in no particular order: better camera, faster processor, better battery, etc. In short, they change their phones because the newer ones offer better and latest features. In most cases, this is triggered by the desire to have a better camera in the phone in terms of higher megapixels.

However, the reality is that higher megapixels in a camera have very limited practical use in a majority of cases. Simply put, higher megapixels mean that the picture file ends up packing more data because of a higher level of detailing. This makes the picture sharper and more importantly, the picture retains its clarity even if enlarged. For example, Apple ran an outdoor hoarding campaign which featured actual pictures taken using an iPhone. These were blown-up to sizes were as high as 20 or 30 feet and the clarity was retained.

Consider the reality that majority of the pictures taken from a phone are either shared online through social media platforms or are saved in the phone or they are backed up somewhere else. A very small percentage of these pictures might be printed and out of that, a miniscule percentage might be printed in sizes larger than a postcard. I cannot imagine an average smartphone user printing any of their pictures in a size which might be 20 feet tall.

Ironically, the pictures which have large file sizes end up being compressed when being shared online in order to save data. Therefore, the net outcome of having a camera with higher megapixels on your phone is that you would require more memory to store these larger-sized files. Larger memory and a higher megapixel camera lead to an increase in the price and the shopper ends up purchasing the same for no significant change or benefit.

What makes these shoppers spend? Trust, faith and nothing else.

Gen X and older shoppers are obviously less informed than the Millennials and they build their trust based on certain rituals which is separate from their faith in the shop itself. For example, shoppers sift through rice, hold it up, sniff at it as well as pop a little into their mouths and chew. If one were to ask them what they were looking for and evaluating, they would not be able to tell clearly. That is because they are following a ritual which reinforces their trust. The actual purchase is based on their trust on the shop and the owner. This ritualized behaviour is only a conscious habit to create an illusion of informed buying.

One can see shoppers knocking on wooden surfaces when purchasing furniture. Again, the question of what was being tested or evaluated would not have a clear answer. The closest response could be some shoppers saying that they were checking if the furniture was durable or not. The extent of their information is that the furniture seems to be solid (usually it means that it is made of wood) or otherwise (which means that it uses particle board).

Shop owners and retailers know the role of trust and its importance in the scheme of things. Most of them actively work at creating, building and also sustaining this trust.

One of the simplest aspects of creating trust is to offer a no-questions-asked return or replacement policy. Since most of the shoppers do know that they might not be making the right decision (this thought is buried deep down inside their minds), anything that can save them from a wrong choice is welcome. No-questions-asked returns or replacement caters to this concern in the shopper's psyche. This is one of the most powerful influences that any neighbourhood shop can employ towards building trust and retaining their shoppers. 'No problem, bring it back' is like a soothing balm to any shopper.

It is no wonder that two of the leading online shopping sites chose to highlight this aspect in a series of advertisements. The interesting characteristic of these advertisements was that both the communications showed a Millennial shopper highlighting how easy it was to exchange or even return the products.

One of these advertisements has an interesting exchange. The elderly shopper comments that he would prefer to purchase from Guptaji's shop because if required he can convince Guptaji to exchange the product. To this the Millennial shopper replies that he can exchange the product on the online site as well and there would be no need to convince anyone. The advertisement explicitly highlights the trust that exists with the neighbourhood shop and points out how the same level of trust is possible with the online site also. Although, the communication addresses one of the key aspects of trust, the actual trust can only be built based on the experience of the shopper.

Therefore, the first step in establishing this trust in the shopper's mind must start with the communication by the retailer. This creates the expectation in the shopper's mind well before they even enter the store or site. Although, the sustainability of this trust lies in consistently meeting the expectations created in the shopper's mind, a retailer leverages a few other aspects to build and reinforce trust and a sense of comfort.

As a shopper you would behave differently in a shop you trust as compared to a store you don't trust. In stores you trust, you will feel subconsciously more relaxed and you will not mind touching and feeling the various products. Next time, when you go shopping, look around for shoppers who are not touching any product and might even be standing back a bit from the display. The chances are that they might leave without any purchases or indulge in some minimal shopping.

Shop owners and retailers know this and leverage this aspect very effectively. A bakery might offer the latest batch of freshly made items for you to taste as soon as you enter. The minute you have tasted even one, the chances of your purchasing something from that bakery shoots up. Even a roadside hawker usually pushes the product into your hands to see and check it out. This is done mainly to get you involved in the transaction. It helps in creating a subconscious level of comfort which leads to trust. Another obvious behaviour is evident in furniture shops. If you are comfortable enough and have a basic or minimum level of trust, you will sit on the sofa, open the wardrobe doors, etc. This engages you as a shopper and nudges you along to the next level of actually considering a purchase. On the other hand, a shopper who is not comfortable will never sit or try out the furniture.

Astute retailers know the power of engagement and a majority of them will give the shopper a basket, bag or trolley near the entrance. This often acts as a subconscious pressure to start purchasing which leads the shopper to touch and experience the products on display. If that cycle is completed, half the job of a retailer is done.

As mentioned earlier, trust is largely based on perception and therefore it is not entirely rational. This makes the shopper susceptible to assumptions and also commit to impulsive transactions. One of the main reasons for customer dissatisfaction is the lack of attention to the fine print or terms and conditions (T&C). The T&C of any retailer is usually drafted from a legal perspective and this is done keeping in mind a worst-case scenario when a dissatisfied customer might take recourse to legal action. In a majority of cases, the shopper hardly ever pays any attention to the T&C which often causes severe dissatisfaction and anger in case of any mismatch between expectation and experience.

An ideal example for this is the delivery time promised by online shopping sites. Most sites usually mention the delivery time as number of 'business days'. This means that the number of days mentioned does not include public holidays and Sundays. Interestingly, when a person places an order, the delivery date mentioned in the final confirmation might be different. These variances are because of a variety of reasons;

it could be for a simple reason that the vendor's location has a public holiday on a different day which has to be factored in.

However, the chances are that a majority of people would register only the number of days and their expectations get defined by the same. Some of the sites have realized this and knowing the importance of creating the right expectations, have started to mention the actual date of the expected delivery instead of a generic number of days on the site.

All these aspects related to trust get linked back to perception and how that has been shaped. The shopper's perception is the only reality they believe in because that has led to trust. If the perception of a shopper is challenged, their trust is shaken and that is a very uncomfortable feeling. On the other hand, when the experience reinforces the perception, the trust level increases and so does the comfort in shopping with that store or site. This is mainly because of the fact mentioned earlier that we shop based more on trust than on rational and logical thinking.

An interaction with a financial advisor is a good example to understand the correlation between trust and perception. Financial advisors are usually representatives of banks, mutual funds, insurance companies, etc. They offer their expertise to help a person plan their finances better and become wealthy. Since this is something everyone wants, they are open to meeting a financial advisor. No one would agree to meet a financial advisor who walks in from the street and offers to provide advice about investments. The role of trust comes into play when a financial institution you trust offers to send a financial advisor. That inherent trust, and a lack of confidence in one's ability to manage one's own finances, provide an opportunity for the financial advisor to step into the picture.

In the course of interactions, if the suggestions being made are diametrically opposite to your perception then the initial trust itself starts to crumble and you would reject the advice as well as the services of such a person. On the other hand, if the suggestions don't challenge your perceptions, you will be inclined to go ahead with the same. If the investments pay off and you get good returns the trust levels increase and your perception about the capability of the financial advisor also increases. Alternatively, if the investments don't turn out well, the trust on the organization might still be intact but your perception about the financial advisor's capability will take a hit.

Now, let me share a reality which might shock most people. The financial advisors most people meet are, by and large, sales persons. Very few of them are actually financially savvy and even fewer have an in-depth knowledge of investments and how they work. They are trained to 'sell' the investment products and as shoppers one 'buys' and invests based on their advice. Is that not dangerous? It is almost as bad as swallowing some chemical because the shopkeeper who is known to you has suggested the same. Yet, this is what a majority of people do based on their trust and the resultant perception.

In fact shopkeepers and retailers adopt a similar approach to manage any dissatisfied customer. If a customer complains about something to the shop owner or manager, the easier solution is to placate the customer by blaming that staff. This might even involve a supposedly angry reprimand and a threat to fire that person. The customer is then reassured that henceforth, the owner or manager will personally attend to their shopping requirements to ensure that such mistakes do not occur again. In most cases it is a win-win situation for everyone. The shopper is happy as their trust is reinforced, the shop owner or manager is happy because the shopper will come back again, and the staff is also happy because they know that nothing much is going to change and they would still be serving the same customer after a few days.

Large retailers and online sites influence this perception and trust factor using a host of sensory elements such as visual cues, music, smell, taste and touch. The example of a bakery offering their freshly made products is a good example of triggering the taste and visual senses to build perception and therefore create trust. I will delve deeper into this in a forthcoming chapter.

This correlation and cyclical link between perception and trust is what makes shopping happen and keep on happening.

As a smart shopper one should first internalize the reality that their shopping is not rational and that trust plays a massive role in their decisions. More importantly, this trust need not be entirely correct. The next level of awareness would be to consciously seek information and objectively evaluate the same with regard to the purchase of any product or service. If practiced diligently, anyone will be able to develop a questioning mind which would help them make shopping decisions in a more logical manner.

At no point in time am I advocating that you should not have trust. On the contrary, trust is very important as that helps in establishing a relationship with the shop which would help you as a shopper. My caution is about blind trust which is not helpful for smart shopping.

### KEY TAKEAWAY

- Trust is the single most important element which defines shopping decisions.
- Shoppers tend to develop trust based on their experiences.
- The experiences must match or exceed the expectations in shoppers' minds for trust to be built.
- Shoppers make purchases based on perception which might not be correct. However, for them, their perception is the reality.
- Perception and trust often make the shoppers overlook or ignore key terms and conditions.

### SMART SHOPPING HABITS

- Develop a questioning mindset with regard to shopping. Don't accept anything at face value.
- Be well informed about the products you purchase. This will minimize the dependence on the shop owner or staff.
- Pay attention to the terms and conditions and other details while shopping. Trust should not make you assume things.

# 3

# I GOT THE BEST PRICE OR DID I?

*What is the right price?*

Ideally, I like to buy a filling, sumptuous packed dinner before entering the airport while flying on one of the low-cost carrier flights. As mentioned earlier, the expectation of free food ceases to exist in a passenger's mind with regard to such airlines. However, the security hassles and the potential mess (literally and figuratively) on my hands deter me from doing this. The alternative to the reheated food available on the flight is to pick up something from the airport which is relatively more expensive than the food I can pick up from outside the airport. The compromising solution would be to buy something at the airport which might be filling and also taste better than what is available on the flight. In absolute money terms, I would pay more for the food picked up at the airport as compared to what would be available outside and it may be marginally less expensive than what I would pay if I purchased food on the flight.

The question is whether I got a good deal at the airport and whether the price I paid for that food is the right price. There are no correct answers to these questions because the whole concept of 'right price' is very nebulous and varies because of multiple parameters.

Price is not equal to value. Value is what shoppers seek and price is only a small part of that. Value is the net outcome of all that a shopper spends in terms of time, money, and effort as compared to what they get in return in terms of the product, shopping experience, service, price, etc. If the net outcome is positive the shopper feels that they have got great value. Alternatively, they feel let down if this outcome is negative. Very clearly, price is just one of the components of this equation. However, it does tend to balance out the equation and deliver a positive outcome in case the other parameters are not satisfactory. For example, a shopper goes into a crowded discount store and tolerates the crowd, the waiting time, etc. in exchange for the low price which becomes the product's value.

Price also has another dimension which is based on your perception.

Suppose you spot a nice garment on sale and it was available for ₹499 as compared to the regular price of ₹999. The chances are that you might purchase that garment and would also be very thrilled with the fact that you got a great deal. A garment you like at a price that is almost half of the original price is definitely something that would delight most shoppers.

However, this thrill and delight might disappear in a second when you meet a friend who has purchased something exactly similar and says that they got it for ₹400 or maybe even less. The first thought to cross your mind would be that what you purchased was of better quality and, therefore, the higher price is worth it. The worst case scenario is when the quality is the same and you feel let-down and cheated because you paid more for the same product.

The same question arises in this context: what is the right price? Is it ₹749 or ₹499 or is it ₹400 or maybe even lower.

This is an interesting conundrum that goes on in the minds of almost every shopper. The key reason for this is the fact that a majority of customers do not know how to assess the quality and, therefore, true worth of what they are buying. They fall back on their trust on the product's brand being purchased or the trust they repose in the shop or retail chain.

This trust creates a perception that the price they are paying is the right value and the product is worth it. This trust is sustained and maintained as long as the shopper is not confronted with an obvious proof to the contrary. In such cases, the shopper starts to look for alternative shops or retail chains and shifts their patronage.

This is what happens when shoppers who have been buying from store A see an advertisement about store B which is selling the same or similar product at a lower price. They might either shift their purchases to store B immediately or after some time when they find that store B is repeatedly offering lower prices. This time taken for a shift would depend on the extent of trust and loyalty as well as the category of the product.

In the case of branded products, the shift from one store to the other might be very soon as the perceived quality (and, therefore, the benefit from purchasing the product) is the same from both the shops. This is one of the key reasons why retail chains as well as online shopping sites highlight the prices of the branded products. However, there is a catch here also and we will come to that in a while.

In case of generic products like grocery, the shift might take longer, if it happens at all. The main reason is due to the fact that shoppers do not know how to evaluate the quality of the products being purchased. They want to believe that they are getting the best deal with their existing shop or store. This trust is central to their shopping and any shopper would resist a challenge to the same as far as possible. This is exactly what happened when the women were told that they were paying more for the rice that they were purchasing which was also of a slightly lower grade. Even if they accepted this at a conscious level, their subconscious would reject the idea that their trusted shop is not giving them the best deal.

How do retailers influence shoppers in such instances and make them shift? This example from a supermarket's initiative holds the answer. The store had massive banners dropping down from the roof and large gas balloons highlighting the price per kilogram of rice. This was visible from far and created an immediate curiosity in the minds of shoppers with regard to the price as it was invariably lower than what they were paying.

This curiosity triggered them to visit the store. In the store, there were three grades of rice: economy, standard and premium. Each of these was competitively priced. In order to publicize the aggressive pricing as well as to bring in new shoppers, the price of the economy grade rice was highlighted. The competitive price and the powerful communication attracted customers in large numbers. The medium of large banners and balloons was so distinctive that customers walked in to the store asking about the banner rice or balloon rice.

Inside the store, all three grades were displayed in bins wherein the customers could derive comfort by sifting through the rice and performing the selection ritual that might comfort them. Subsequently, when they noticed the other grades and the comparison to the market prices, they often ended up upgrading their purchase. However, the hook which pulled them to the store was the lowest price of the economy grade rice.

Several aspects played an important part in this. The sheer size of the banner or balloon was obviously relevant. Also, the price was always printed in block red font and it was mentioned in terms of per kilogram of rice. Red has a very strong psychological and physiological impact which will be detailed in the next chapter. The price mentioned was 'per kilogram' and it was easy to use as a reference since the shopper would remember the price point of his or her current purchase in per kilogram terms as well.

The other dimension to price perception is quality. Since shoppers cannot accurately judge the quality of the products they are purchasing, they tend to link price to quality. That is, they define the quality they want and are comfortable with in terms of the price they have to pay. They do not do this with regard to the quality parameters by itself.

Let us examine this in the context of jeans as an example. This is a fairly universal garment, and almost everyone purchases and wears jeans. If a diverse group of people was asked to define the quality or type of jeans they purchased, the response would either be in terms of brand names or as a price band. Some of them might purchase jeans in the price range of ₹500–₹750, some in the range of ₹1,000–₹1,500, a few might purchase jeans worth ₹1,500–₹2,500 and there might be shoppers who would only buy jeans which are ₹2,500 and above. Each of these price bands are referred to as price points. In simple terms, shoppers' expectations are linked to the quality available at that particular price.

As a shopper, your reference point for an acceptable quality is expressed in terms of such a price point. This is all the more relevant for generic categories like grocery where the presence of brands is limited. Since the link to quality perception is based on the price point, a shopper is also very suspicious of any offer where the retailer might claim to sell a pair of jeans worth ₹2,500 for ₹750 or a kilogram of rice worth ₹50 for ₹20. This doubt arises because of the complex interplay of a few factors in the mind of a shopper such as the trust factor in the existing store, inability to judge the quality independently, etc.

However, if the competitor is smart and understands the shopper's psyche well, they will offer a price differential which is significant enough to attract the attention of the shopper and trigger their interest while it is also well within a believable price point range or price band. Otherwise the shopper will end up rejecting the price or discount by assuming that something is wrong with the products or that this is a one-time gimmick.

Interestingly, there is a major limitation with regard to this price perspective in the minds of shoppers. This limitation pertains to the extent of prices that any shopper can remember and recall. From the vast number of products that are usually purchased, any shopper can recall the approximate prices of only a handful of products. These would be products that they purchase frequently or those products that they spend a significant amount of money on. In the case of grocery, shoppers might be able to recall the price points that they are habituated to and are comfortable with such as rice, wheat, oil, etc. Even in the case of vegetables which are purchased frequently, a shopper might not recall the price trends of all the vegetables but he will be able to recall the price points of onions, tomatoes and potatoes because these are purchased regularly.

It is no wonder then that the rising price of onions is always a cause of alarm and even the government steps in to manage instances when it skyrockets above a particular level. Governments at the State and even the Centre have been under threat because of a sharp rise in onion prices. It is reported that the late Mrs Indira Gandhi used the rising prices of onions as a major plank to stage a comeback in the 1980 general elections. Retailers also know the power of onions as well as of similar such products.

These products are referred to as 'Known Value Items' (KVI) for obvious reasons. These are products whose value and related price point is known to the shopper and hence it becomes an easy reference point for them.

It is precisely for the same reason that retailers use these KVI products to influence the price perception and hence attempt to undermine the trust of the shopper in the store that they frequent regularly. Check out the prices on some of the advertisements by retail stores and chains and you will be able to relate to this easily.

In 2010, when the prices of onions spiked to unbelievable levels, the power of this vegetable as a KVI came to the fore. In the supermarket chain I was associated with, we had an offer where we were selling onions at almost half the price of what was being quoted in the market. The caveat was that this special price was applicable only to those shoppers who purchased for a minimum value; also, the quantity of onions at this special price was limited per shopper. I am positive that this promotional offer helped bring in a lot of new customers as well as retain them.

Retailers leverage the price perception to get the shoppers' attention and make them visit the store. Once inside, the customers might start to trust the store based on their shopping experience. Advertisements with pictures of KVI products with low prices, special offers, etc., are all a part of that plan.

Several retail chains and a few online sites have even tried to guarantee that their price is the lowest. This is backed with a promise that if the shopper is able to provide a bill as the proof that they got the same product elsewhere for a lower price, the shopper would get the difference in price or sometimes even double that amount returned to him. The reality is that this does not work out especially in India where the concept of maximum retail price (MRP) prevails. There are various reasons, related to MRP, why offering a price guarantee would be very challenging for a retailer. Thus, it would suffice to say that it is not so easy to implement.

On the other hand, the stipulation that a shopper should get a bill from the other retailer as the proof for lower price is self-defeating for many of the high-priced products. Also, no shopper would go through the trouble of obtaining the proof for lower priced products. However, as a promise, it does work on creating a perception which helps to build the shopper's trust with regard to pricing.

A low price guarantee or assurance is definitely possible for a shorter time frame and/or for specific products. This is a regular practice we see in India, especially in the consumer durables and electronics category. During the New Year period, most consumer durables and electronics stores offer special sales which are usually positioned as Lowest Price Guarantee, Zero Margin Sale, etc.

There is an interesting story behind the genesis of this practice which was started by a leading consumer durables retailer in Chennai.

The period between mid-December to mid-January is a period called Margazhi in Tamilian calendar and it is somewhat similar to the Shradh period observed in northern India. Margazhi is supposed to be a month dedicated to spiritual pursuits, devotion and prayer. Weddings are not conducted during this period and usually any materialistic activity is also avoided during this month.

This period comes after a shopping splurge during Dusshera and Diwali, and it is usually a low sale period for retailers. The sentimental and traditional aspect of Margazhi ended up having a significant dent on the sales of product categories like consumer durables and electronics. Lack of wedding-related purchases coupled with people not making even routine purchases for their home led to a very sharp decline in sales and usually left the retailers and manufacturers with large inventory levels at the end of the year.

One retailer decided to do something about this drop in sales in the late '70s and started the concept of a 'New Year Sale' which offered the best deals of the year. The sale was for three days in the initial few years, on the 30 and 31 of December, and the 1 of January. Advertisements and adequate publicity created enough interest and led to massive crowds who were keen to get the best deals. The previous conditioning of Margazhi went out the window and one could see hordes of shoppers making a beeline for the store. This idea grew to such an extent that the retailer had to arrange for separate premises in order to manage the crowds.

Like with all good things, imitation followed and soon every consumer durables store started having the year-end sale in some form or the other. As mentioned earlier, all these sales were termed as 'Cost Price Sale', 'Zero Margin Sale', etc. The positioning of this sale was done in such a manner as to leverage the perception of the statement: cost price or zero margins. After all, who would not like to buy products at the cost price!

The next step was to try and outdo each other by starting the sale earlier. Nowadays, these sales kick off from the 25 of December and go on till the 1 or 2 of January. Needless to say, every store selling this category of products has to have this year-end sale since it has become a default expectation of the shopper. Therefore, the brand owners and manufacturers are also actively involved in this sale and support various stores in different ways.

These sales rest on the basic concept of 'Loss Leaders'. Loss leaders are the products which are highlighted as being sold at cost price, with zero margin, etc. Since these products would have very low prices, they would be an attractive buy. However, the retailer rarely incurs any losses on such sales.

I know of many shoppers who undertake what I like to call as an expedition during this year-end sale. Their endeavour is as much a routine as the sale itself. Armed with a list of things that they would like to buy, they go around checking the prices of the products across various retailers who are having a sale. Finally, they decide and purchase the product and most probably they go and purchase the product from the store they normally frequent. This would also have been the first store they went in to check the price.

Needless to say, these shoppers would largely be from the older generation or Gen X. The Millennials might participate in such sales for generic products like a battery pack or if a new and latest product is available on sale. The same orientation is seen in online shopping sites that frequently organize flash sales. If you would notice, the products on such flash sales are predominantly categories which would appeal more to the Millennial shoppers.

The reason why shoppers end up coming back and purchasing from the first and their regular store is simply because of the fact that no shopper is able to find the exact same model on sale with any other retailer. This is because the manufacturers along with retailers use this opportunity to do two things.

First is to liquidate the unsold inventory of products or models which have not been selling as much as expected. The second and related objective is to try and sell out models which are no longer being manufactured. These are called 'End of Life' models and they need to be sold as newer models are either about to enter the market or have already been launched.

In that context, the manufacturer offers each of the retailers or chains one of these models at very attractive terms. This, in turn, enables the retailer to sell these products at very low prices during the sale and yet make money. Since they are perceived to be making a loss in the sale of such products, the term Loss Leaders has come into use. The additional benefit that retailers get from such sales is twofold.

First is that they are able to reinforce trust in the minds of their shoppers with regard to offering the best deal and maximum value. The reality that the exact model with same features is not available anywhere else is something that no shopper registers. The lingering thought is that their regular retailer does seem to offer the lowest price or the best deal.

The second benefit is that retailers often keep newer models and other products which are not on sale as part of the display. There is a percentage of shoppers who are motivated to check out these products and change their purchasing plan to pick up something which is not on sale. This is an added sale and, of course, increases the margins for the retailer.

The 'End of Season Sale' (EOSS) that one sees in almost every lifestyle store a few times a year is also based on the very same rationale.

As I have often mentioned, shopping is not rational. It is the most emotional, impulsive and irrational activity which is justified by the shopper based on their influences. Chasing the best bargain or value for money is another example of this perspective with regard to shopping.

When a shopper is going to various stores in search of the best price as well as to compare prices, they tend to overlook one very important aspect—that is the cost of doing this comparison. Both, the absolute money spent because of fuel costs and the time cost is never considered. If one were to factor in these elements, no shopper would go to check prices across stores.

However, the need to check prices and get the best deal is extremely compulsive for any shopper. In today's Internet and smartphone environment, this tends to be easier and can even be done with minimal or no cost. However, the accuracy of information available online cannot be guaranteed every time and that tends to make the older generation as well as the Gen Xers prefer physical visits to check the prices.

Even the Millennials, who constitute a large percentage of online shoppers, find it difficult to compare prices because of the differences in models and features. One of the main reasons for a high level of dissatisfaction and complaints about used products being sent to online shoppers stem from the lack of checking the details and focusing solely on the price factor. In several instances, the vendor on the site was actually offering only a second-hand product which the shopper did not register as he/she was focused on the price alone. This is similar to the dissatisfaction with regard to the delivery time simply because the shopper did not register the term 'business days'.

In most cases, online sites have realized this and have stopped allowing any vendor from offering second-hand products. They now focus on communicating 'only original products' in some of their advertisements.

Since shoppers tend to focus primarily on prices and it forms an integral part of their perception about a store, retailers use another aspect of pricing in order to build trust. It is called price cues and refers to the prices being set at 9,99,999, etc. The reality is that one rupee is not going to make any difference, especially in today's context; yet, shoppers usually register the price as being below 10 or 100 or 1,000. It is a psychological trick that our mind falls for quite regularly. In India, we also refer to this kind of pricing as Bata pricing since Bata footwear stores have traditionally followed this style of pricing for their products. The interesting reality is that in spite of this being so obvious and almost everyone being aware of the same, price cues still continue to impact the price perception of shoppers.

Let us now get back to our earlier example of store A and store B where a shopper shifts to store B because of lower prices being communicated. This could be because of KVIs or lost leaders, etc. Suppose store A started advertising that they offer an even lower price than store B, what will the shopper do now?

The answer might be obvious that the shopper would shift back to store A. However, that might not be the case. The construct of perception and trust in a shopper's mind is very complex. In such a scenario, the shopper would immediately doubt as to why store A did not offer this lower price in the first instance. So, instead of influencing the perception in a positive manner, the advertisement has now filled the shopper's mind with doubt. If the price differential is significant, the shopper might shift their purchase to store A, but whether they continue with store A or store B would be dependent on several other factors. In most cases, the stores end up competing with each other about prices and promotional offers. This has also led to a shopping behaviour called 'cherry picking'.

'Cherry picking' refers to shoppers who go to various stores and purchase only those products which have the best offers and lowest prices. This is counterproductive for retailers as they need to constantly give very attractive offers to bring in the shoppers. Shoppers are savvy and quickly figure this out. Once this pattern becomes established, shoppers would keep shifting or cherry picking amongst the retailers thereby forcing them to give aggressive discounts and offers.

The EOSS is a great example of this pattern. I know of many shoppers who wait for the EOSS and purchase only during the sale. Similar is the case with online sites and their approach to discounts and flash sales. Shoppers tend to swing between various sites based on the best deal and over a period of time this erodes long-term shopper loyalty.

A recent incident involving an online classified site is a

classic example to illustrate how savvy shoppers can be. This site offered free transportation of products listed and sold on their site. It also offered some cashback in the form of credit for an e-wallet site. One shopper wanted to shift his house and hit upon an idea to do this without any cost. He listed the products on this site and sold them to his spouse who had a different mobile number and whose address was their new residence. The team from the classified site promptly came and shifted the belongings and also gave a credit on the e-wallet towards the cashback. This person then used a cab from one of the app-based cab operators and paid that person from the e-wallet amount. Thus, he shifted incurring zero cost! This story was doing the rounds on social media for quite some time.

As a smart shopper, it does make sense to be aware of and evaluate the best deal in terms of price. However, smart shoppers also know that price is not the only parameter in shopping and they do not give it undue importance. The most crucial aspect is to be aware and conscious of the price point vis-à-vis the related quality that one is seeking. This requires some amount of product knowledge and the efforts towards that will be well worth it.

One of the critical aspects of focusing too much on price is the tendency to purchase more than what is required or planned. As a smart shopper, one should be aware that even after a discount, any additional purchase is not a saving at all. In fact, when a shopper tends to be focused on the price, they end up missing out on checking various other aspects and might actually end up getting a bad deal.

## KEY TAKEAWAY

- There is no universally correct, right price.
- Price is not the same as value. Price is only a small element which makes up the perception of value in a shopper's mind.
- Shoppers seek value and often mistake low prices for great value. This is incorrect.
- During the sale season, it is not worth going around comparing prices as the exact same products/models are rarely on sale.

## SMART SHOPPING HABITS

- Remember that there is no universal right price. Price is relative to the expectation of quality.
- Research and get information as well as details about the products to be purchased. This would help in determining the correct price point.
- Use the Internet and smartphones for searching. However, be prudent in trusting whatever you see online.
- Be aware of your preferred price point and try to stick to the same.
- Male shoppers should learn to bargain in order to become smart shoppers.

# 4

# THE LADY IN RED

*Sense and sensibility*

'The Lady in Red' is a 1980s song by British-Irish singer-songwriter Chris de Burgh. The lyrics of the song go like this:

> I've never seen you looking so lovely as you did tonight
> I've never seen you shine so bright
> I've never seen so many men ask you if you wanted to dance
> They're looking for a little romance, given half a chance
> And I have never seen that dress you're wearing
> Or the highlights in your hair that catch your eyes
> I have been blind
> The lady in red is dancing with me, cheek to cheek…

The song became a huge hit and was a part of most playlists. I recall wondering as to why the colour red was used in the song? Why not blue or purple or for that matter any other colour? Blue was my preferred option and it is not surprising because most men tend to like blue and name it as their favourite colour. Over the years, I have seen red used to signify passion, danger, etc. The question of why the colour red was chosen in the song was on my mind for many years until my retail experience gave me the answer.

Meanwhile, I was also checking out whether other colours have been used in any song in a similar context and in conjunction with a lady. I did discover another song which was in fact older and not as famous as 'The Lady in Red'. This song, 'Lady in Blue', is a song from the 1970s and was sung by an Irish singer named Joe Dolan. The lyrics go like this:

> Who's that lady on her own
> I wish that she would look my way
> She just stands there on her own
> A painted smile upon her face
> Lonely lady dressed in blue
> May I have this dance with you
> Let me hold you in my arms
> Let the music fill your heart…

It is interesting to see the feelings communicated in these two songs where two different colours were associated with a lady. The song using the colour red has strong words which evoke passion and brightness, and it is very upbeat. The other song that uses the colour blue is a direct opposite in terms of the lyrics at least. It creates a sense of loneliness, melancholy and is definitely not upbeat. In fact a few studies have shown that both men and women tend to feel a higher level of attraction when a person of the opposite gender wears red. There are various explanations and theories regarding this and we will come to that shortly.

The question arises whether these two songwriters used red or blue colours based on the mood of the song, or the mood of the song end up being distinctly different because of the choice of respective colours?

The answer points towards how our senses can be influenced, imagery can be evoked and our psyche can be manipulated through various such elements. Let me start with the visual characteristics first and how it influences us, especially as shoppers.

Our sight is one of the key factors which validate our thoughts and beliefs. We tend to believe something we see and that is precisely what illusionists and magicians leverage to trick our senses. One of the greatest magicians, Harry Houdini, is supposed to have performed mind-boggling illusions which include the act of making an elephant vanish from inside one of the largest theatres in New York in 1918. Of course, the reality is obvious that the elephant did not disappear but was hidden in plain sight. However, the audience believed that the elephant had vanished because that is what they saw and therefore wanted to believe.

Almost every magician's act involves a lot of talk, gesticulating, pointing, etc. All these are planned and practised to perfection to ensure that the eyes of the audience get glued on to this movement while the actual 'magic' of making things vanish or appear is happening quietly on the side. Take a simple real-life scenario where you are deeply engrossed in some task or thought and then suddenly, when your concentration shifts, you notice a change which earlier did not even register in your mind. Someone could have come in quietly and stood before you and then when you focus, it appears like the person has appeared there by magic.

Optical illusions are a reality in life and our eyes which define what we choose to believe can be deceived far more easily than we think. Therefore, what we see might not be real but it definitely influences our perception and for every person their perception is their reality.

Colours play a significant role in creating perceptions just like in the two songs mentioned in the beginning of this chapter.

Welcome to the power and influence of colours over our mind and body.

We tend to associate colours with emotions and other imagery since our childhood. As I mentioned, most men choose blue as their favourite colour. Interestingly, a significant number of women also choose blue as their favourite colour but not as many as men. The second-most favourite colour for women is purple which will not find any place in the list of favourite colours for men. What factors influences these choices and preferences have been the subject of many studies and is a vast topic in itself. One thought is that the colours and their imagery are linked to the context in which we see the colours in nature and the environment around us.

Apart from creating a perception because of the imagery they evoke, colours are also supposed to have an actual physiological influence on a person.

Everyone must have heard of VIBGYOR which is an acronym for the colours seen in a rainbow: Violet, Indigo, Blue, Green, Yellow, Orange and Red. The combination of all these colours creates white and the absence of them is black. In reality, white light is broken up into these seven colours and when there is no light and hence no colours, it is black. Rainbows are nothing but the breakup of white light because of the prism-like effect of rain drops. That is why a rainbow is always opposite to the sun's position. The colours which make up the white light have different wavelengths that influence their impact.

Red has the longest wavelength in the colour spectrum. It can be seen from afar and also ends up appearing a bit closer than it is in reality. This is because, in simple terms, colours with longer wavelengths travel further than those with shorter wavelengths because they take a relatively longer time to disperse in air. The use of red colour for signals, as danger signs and also for emergency services could be because of this fact.

Apart from this, red also tends to have an actual physiological effect on people. It increases the pulse rate which creates a sense of urgency. Similarly, yellow is also a very stimulating colour and is supposed to increase alertness and even the rate of metabolism. However, yellow also tends to create a sense of unease or anger because of its brightness. It is no coincidence that one of the world's largest fast-food chains uses a colour scheme following the combination of red and yellow.

The logic is related to what the outlet wants as the expected customer behaviour. Being a fast-food outlet, they want the customers to order a lot, eat fast as well as move out fast so that more customers can be served in the same time period. A combination of red and yellow is possibly the best option to achieve this objective because of the physiological effects these colours have.

Green actually relaxes our muscles and it is soothing to the eye. We are also surrounded by a lot of green in nature and, therefore, this colour triggers association with being natural, healthy, fresh, etc. The use of green in the vegetable section of stores as well as in places providing healthcare is not an accident; it actually is helpful in such places by visually inducing a sense of calm and well being.

Blue is a direct opposite to red in terms of physiological effects. It reduces the pulse rate which relaxes a person. The association of blue also evokes the imagery of sky which makes it a very soothing colour. Similarly, violet or purple are also calming colours and are associated with luxury.

The association of purple with luxury is because this colour has always been linked with royalty. It is due to the simple reason that purple dye was made from a mollusc which was found only in a specific region of the Mediterranean Sea. Since a large number of sea creatures were required to make the dye, it was extremely expensive. Hence, only the royalty could afford fabrics dyed in purple. This led to the imagery of luxury that purple evokes till date.

However, one must also keep in mind that the association and imagery of colours are also influenced by culture and local customs. The best example is that black is considered inauspicious in India and would never feature in any auspicious occasion.

Retailers know the impact of colours on shoppers and a lot of detailed thought goes into designing a store and selecting the colour schemes. One common colour used by all retailers in varying degrees is red, for obvious reasons. Every sale- or offer-related communication invariably uses red to leverage the effect of the colour on the shopper as well as to ensure that it can be seen from far. It is very common for shoppers to spot a SALE sign in bright red and then decide to go to that store.

Colours are visible because of light and that is an important design element in any store in order to influence shopping behaviour. If you have purchased or accompanied someone purchasing the traditional South Indian silk sari or *Pattu* sari, you will notice an interesting behaviour pattern. Experienced shoppers would take the shortlisted saris to a window or near the door to check the colour of the sari. This is a very important aspect as the shade of the sari might look different under different kinds of light.

Without getting too technical, there is the cool white light like the light from a tubelight and the warm yellow light, from a traditional bulb. Both these kinds of lighting have their own applications and uses. Cool white light is ideal for general lighting where the intent is more about creating enough illumination to be comfortable and easy visibility. On the other hand, a yellow light creates a sense of warmth and is typically used in those areas where such a sensory aspect is required. Brightness is a key factor and the level is adjusted depending on the effect required. Next time you go to any store and if you tend to move towards any part of the store subconsciously, stop and check; the chances are that the area has relatively brighter lighting which attracts shoppers. The reverse is also true; dark spots as well as extremely bright areas might not have many shoppers.

Spotlights highlighting a display play a dual role; attracting your attention and accentuating the products on display. The key mistake which many stores in India make is to go overboard with lighting. This is particularly seen in jewellery and clothing stores. Apart from hurting the eyes, such excessive lighting makes the store warmer which increases the air-conditioning usage leading to higher electricity bills.

It is not only lighting and colours but also the text or wording which adds to the impact on a shopper. 'Sale' or 'Free' tends to be like a red flag to a bull (pun intended). Shoppers rush into a store which has such posters. Other words like 'Rush', 'Limited Stock', 'Special', etc. are also used to create a subconscious sense of urgency in shoppers' minds. This is because these words tend to convey that if shoppers do not purchase immediately, they will lose out on a fabulous opportunity. The next chapter will explore this facet in greater detail.

Equally important in the context of visual influences is how the products are displayed. If you have noticed, supermarkets or hypermarkets have bins filled with a product and a sign about an offer. The haphazard filling of the bin again reinforces the imagery that if the shopper did not rush and pick up these products they will miss out on a great deal. Imagine if these products had been kept in a well-arranged manner. The sense of chaos and the feeling of being rushed would obviously not be there.

The same visual impact is also leveraged while planning the product display, for instance, which products should be kept on which shelf as well as where should they be displayed inside a store. Invariably leading brands are always displayed above or below the eye level. The spaces at eye level are always used to display products that the retailer would like to promote in a subtle manner. As shoppers search for leading brands they first see and notice the other brands kept at their eye level. There is a chance that they might change their minds and end up picking up a product displayed at the eye level instead of the leading brand they had originally wanted. This is aptly described in a Hindi statement, '*Jo dikhta hain, who bikta hain*' which translates to what is seen, is sold.

Therefore, even a simple visual act is also an important sensory influence. Seeing the product display creates an impact on our minds. The pictures that are put up, the mannequins that are displayed, every aspect plays on the visual aspect and influences our shopping. A related example is the use of open kitchens in many restaurants. This is done to create a visual impact to build up anticipation about the food and subconsciously reinforce trust by showcasing a neat and clean kitchen.

While on the topic of restaurants, what happens to a person when they walk into a café or a bakery and the smell of coffee or freshly baked items hits our senses? Invariably the person starts salivating without even being aware of the same. That is the power of smell which is the next strong sensory influence. Most people do not realize that smell not only appeals to our conscious minds but is also a powerful trigger for our subconscious memories. A simple experiment would be to close your eyes and smell a baby powder while focusing on how you feel and the thoughts that come to your mind. The chances are that you will feel a sense of gentleness and images associated with babies will fill your mind.

The use of smell to influence shoppers is still at a very nascent stage. Most retailers still only focus on eliminating bad smells and having some kind of a mild perfumed environment. However, the opportunity to influence shoppers through the sense of smell is immense. It is a validated fact that shoppers in a pleasant smelling store tend to shop more. Several international stores use a specific fragrance which is often especially made for them to leverage this sensory influence. There are aerosol dispensers or mechanisms connected to the air conditioning which can spray fragrances that range from the smell of wet earth to cut grass, and various types of coffee or floral scents, all of which create a sensory impact on you without you being aware of the same. Home improvement stores in the USA often use the fragrance of freshly cut grass as it immediately creates an association with hard work, home, etc.

The interesting reality of using smell is that it is dependent on culture. For example, the smell of freshly cut grass in India would have very little effect on any shopper, apart from creating a sense of freshness. This is because Indian consumers are not DIY (Do It Yourself) consumers. This means that they rarely do any repair, maintenance work at home, and instead depend on electricians, carpenters, gardeners, etc., Since our cultural context does not expose us to smells associated with home repair or maintenance work, the smell of cut grass does not have a strong association for us. In contrast, an American shopper would associate it with hard work, home, etc., because most of the homeowners do things like mowing their lawns themselves.

The power of smell is also used in the perfume section of any lifestyle store with the sales person spraying the various perfumes on small strips of paper for customers to check. Many perfume sections also keep a cup of fresh coffee beans and encourage shoppers to smell the beans before checking out the perfumes. This is to ensure that the shoppers' sense of smell is neutralized and they can smell the next perfume properly without any other conflicting smell.

The next sensory aspect is our hearing. It also has a role to play, although not as significant a one as played by the visual aspect or the smell. Music has an impact on our mood and that is a well-known fact. The tempo of music influences our perspective. Slow, melodious, instrumental music creates a mellow mood and is ideal for lifestyle stores whereas fast-paced, loud music helps in mass merchandise stores such as supermarkets or hypermarkets. This is linked to the pre-existing state of mind of a shopper when he goes to a store. When someone is shopping for lifestyle products, they would like to browse and check out various options and a mellow mood complements that thought and vice versa.

Interestingly enough, the Millennials are supposed to be able to tolerate loud and fast music as compared to the earlier generations. This could be due to their preference to certain music genres or linked to their habitual use of headphones. Regardless of the reason, this also indicates that music has to be tailored for the shopper's generational influence and what might work for one age group would fail with another.

Touch is another aspect in the set of sensory influences and one of the key reasons why shoppers prefer self-service stores. Shoppers feel free when allowed to touch and feel the product and this enables them to be more involved in the shopping process. Shoppers purchasing from traditional shops which are over-the-counter and where the shopkeeper needs to take out the products and pass them on to the customers cannot influence the touch aspect. 'Touch, Feel and See' are the three key elements of any self-service store and that is also the key driver for impulse purchases. It has been proven that shoppers end up buying 30 per cent or more than what they had planned to purchase in self-service stores. Although these impulse-led purchases are influenced by all the sensory elements, the aspect of touch plays a crucial part in this. Touch is also indicative of the trust factor as mentioned earlier and that adds to the overall impact.

The last of the sensory aspects used to influence shoppers is taste. This is predominantly applicable in stores selling food and related products. The simplest way to influence taste is to offer food products as samples to the shoppers. Many international retailers do this consistently as the products that have been given for sampling see an immediate spurt in sales.

It is quite difficult to overcome sensory influences because there is a complex interplay among all the five senses. Also, these influences operate largely at a subconscious level. It is precisely because of these reasons that shopper research is now expanding into newer frontiers.

Retailers are constantly studying shopper-behaviour and their responses to various stimuli in a shop or site. Shopper-behavioural studies are now focusing more on understanding the subconscious responses and brain activity since traditional surveys and focus groups tend to reveal only what is in the conscious mind. However, the subconscious determines the majority of a person's responses and it is often faster than the conscious thought. Since shopping is largely influenced by the subconscious mind, shopper studies are nowadays even using procedures such as Functional Magnetic Resonance Imaging (FMRI) or Electroencephalography (EEG) to understand how the brain responds to stimuli during shopping.

This has even led to a new area of focus which is called Neuromarketing. However, there have also been various issues and concerns about privacy, manipulation, etc., about such studies and this debate is only bound to increase.

Simply put, the main influence during shopping is a chemical called Dopamine. This is a neurotransmitter or, in other words, it is like a messenger which helps in the transmission of signals. Although the details about this chemical and its actions are extremely complex and it has myriad effects on our brain and body, one aspect is very relevant to the topic of shopping. I am not medically qualified to expound on Dopamine and thus, will only share my limited understanding of its influence on shopping behaviour.

Dopamine is supposed to be closely linked to the reward centre of our brain which drives positive feelings, i.e., the part of the brain which makes us feel good, satiated, satisfied, etc. It is clearly one of the reasons why a person feels good after a filling meal. Thus, low levels of this chemical makes a person feel dull, fatigued, etc., and any activity which increases the level of this chemical becomes associated with a positive emotion like pleasure. On the flip side, it is also linked to addiction that leads to thrill-seeking, risky behaviour as it tends to boost the level of it chemical in a person's system.

Retail therapy is a term often used for someone who does shopping when he or she is feeling depressed and down. In reality, what the person is doing is indulging in an activity which increases the levels of Dopamine and subsequently improves his or her mood. Over a period of time, this association leads to a behavioural pattern of wanting to shop when feeling down. The level of Dopamine and its association with reward in our minds is a very strong trigger for our impulsive behaviour while shopping especially with regard to promotional offers. The effect of promotions on shopping is what we will discuss in the next chapter.

A smart shopper would have to first become aware of all these sensory influences and that in itself is a big step. The next step would be to manage these influences and to, some extent, control the subconscious, impulsive responses triggered by them. These responses can be controlled and contained by our rational and conscious thoughts. However, the rational part of our brain requires some time to process the information and respond. That is why smart shoppers would not react immediately to stimuli but think about it and then act only if required. In such a scenario, one would be able to minimize the impulsive responses to a large extent. Although, this is not easy, it is also not impossible.

The reality is that these impulsive responses are also influenced by the level of a chemical in our brains. Although, controlling it might be difficult, there are some simple tips to ensure that the level of this neurotransmitter is not too low. Simple things like eating, especially a ripe banana, exercising, etc., might keep these levels in check.

## KEY TAKEAWAY

- The five sensory influences trigger powerful responses as they impact the subconscious.
- Colours affect us physiologically as well as create strong imageries.
- Visual impact is leveraged through display of products that encourages purchase.
- Smell is the most powerful emotionally-linked sense because it automatically triggers subconscious memories associated with a particular smell.
- Shoppers prefer self-service stores as they enable the 'Touch, Feel and See' experience. This is one of the key factors that drive, impulse buying.

## SMART SHOPPING HABITS

- Be aware of the impact of these sensory elements.
- Curb the tendency to react impulsively to any of these sensory influences.
- Allow the rational mind to process the information and help you take a logical decision.
- If you wish to limit your shopping, consciously avoid touching the products on display.
- Exercise before shopping; it would tire you as well as increase your Dopamine levels.
- Eat before shopping, preferably ripe bananas.
- If you feel the need to indulge in some retail therapy, stick to window shopping at those stores which are not open.

# 5

# FREE IS GOD!

The power of promotions and offers

Having opened many stores over the years as part of a management team of several retail chains, I have learnt one undeniable fact: that is the enormous power and influence of promotional offers on shoppers.

Without sounding condescending, the fact remains that the words Sale, Free, etc. are guaranteed to attract a horde of shoppers. It is no wonder that retailers use such terms 'Free is God' to describe the extent of their influence.

Let me share some interesting instances to explain the various dimensions of how promotional offers influence a shopper.

I am sure that you have purchased health drinks just because of a free bat or ball which came along with it. The net result of all these purchases could very well be that the various bats or balls have been used, lost or broken while many of the health drink bottles are still taking up space in your kitchen shelves.

Let me give you a contradictory example of a freebie offer which did not have many takers. Freebie is a term used by retailers for any promotional offer which offers something free. A large consignment of talcum powder was purchased because it was available at a very low special price. Apart from selling the same, the store decided to offer it as a freebie to any customer who purchased more than a particular value. Initially, there was a lot of interest and many shoppers actually purchased more in order to get this free talcum powder. However, after a few weeks the shopper response started to change and customers started to refuse the free talcum powder and in a few instances even wanted discount equivalent to the price of that product. Finally, the situation was such that shoppers just refused to take the free product; meanwhile, the sales of that talcum powder also dropped drastically.

What was the problem? Why did shoppers respond to this promotional offer in such a dramatically different manner? Does this mean that 'Free' is not as much of an influencer as everyone thinks it is?

For the answer, I will first deconstruct what 'free' means in the mind of a shopper and hence its power to influence the shopper-behaviour.

Everyone likes to get something for nothing. It is a universal behaviour and that is what free is all about. The key word in the statement is 'something' and it has to be of value for the freebie to be meaningful.

As mentioned in an earlier chapter, value is the sum total of all that a shopper expends versus the sum total of everything that he perceives to get in return. So, the perception of what he is getting in return is very crucial. If his perception about the free product is not very positive, then there is no value and therefore the free product loses its power to influence shopping-behaviour.

In the case of a ball or a bat, the value perception in the mind of a child is always very high. No child will ever tire of getting yet another ball, bat or any other thing to play. Therefore, a free ball or a bat will always attract the shopper because of the perennial attraction of the free product. However, in the case of the talcum powder, the perceived value of the product dropped very soon and hence the free product lost its power to influence.

As shoppers you would have come across several instances where there is a free product being offered but you are not interested in the same. Typically, shoppers demand a discount proportionate to the price of the free item and this request is invariably not entertained. There is a very simple reality behind this. The free products given are often sourced in bulk as part of a special deal. Hence, the cost of such free items is very low as compared to their MRP or selling price. That is the main reason why retailers will not give discounts instead of the free item. The other reason is if the retailer ended up giving discounts instead of the free product, most customers would prefer a discount and the retailer would be left behind with a huge quantity of the free item. In a few cases, where the retailer agrees to give a discount instead of the free product, the value of the discount will be far less than the perceived value of the free item.

Suppose there was a free DVD player being given along with an LCD television and you did not want it as you already have a very good DVD player. What should you do in such a scenario? It is better to take the DVD player and then use it as a gift than to try and negotiate for a discount in lieu of the DVD player because the discount might be a fraction of the player's actual price. But, if you take the player and use it as a gift, the perceived value of that gift would be far higher than the discount you would have got.

Let us now get back to how retailers identify the right product to be given as a freebie and which item would have the highest value perception in a shopper's mind.

There are three dimensions to this aspect: relevance of the free product to the purchase, value of the free product and the utility of the free product.

As part of the Independence Day promotions in 2014, a

leading consumer durables chain had a very different kind of promotional offer in their advertisement. They were offering an interesting mix of products with LED televisions of 32 inches and above. The choice of the products being offered as freebies was 2 kilogram each of tur dal and urad dal, 5 kilogram each of rice, atta and sugar plus one litre of Sunflower cooking oil. Essentially, they were offering a mix of grocery items which every household would use. Prima facie, it would appear to be a good idea especially when the prices of these grocery items are in triple digits. The fact also remains that the television is purchased for the home and grocery is also used in the home. One can even stretch his or her imagination to a scenario where the family would eat a meal made from these items and watch the television, therefore creating a connection.

Regardless of how many scenarios anyone can think about, this was a bad idea with a capital B. However, I have learnt over my years of retail experience that shoppers change and they can surprise or even shock you with their expectations. Therefore, to validate my view that it was a bad idea based on my understanding of shopper-behaviour, I shared information about this offer in a few forums. I sought feedback and comments from shoppers about whether they found such an offer to be of interest and did they perceive value in it. The majority rejected the idea. Next, I checked with the retail chain and found that this promotional offer had bombed.

The key reason why this did not work and was a bad idea from the start pertains to the lack of relevance and value perceived by the shoppers. Although the utility value of the freebie for any shopper was very high, the absence of relevance led to its failure.

The concept of relevance in the shopper's perception as well as in the actual shopping activity is very crucial. This is the reason why stores tend to display products grouped in similar categories and more importantly they do not mix up the categories.

For example, if you were in a lifestyle store and purchasing apparel would you be open to buying detergent too? Logically speaking, there is a very close correlation and relevance between detergents and clothing. Yet, very few shoppers would even consider buying such a product when shopping for apparel or clothing. The reason goes back to the subconscious thinking patterns and is linked to the usage of product categories. Shoppers tend to compartmentalize products based on their usage. Thus, when shopping for one type of usage, their minds would usually exclude products which are not linked to that particular usage. Therefore, the shoppers' value perception of any freebie is clearly defined by this compartmentalization. If shoppers do not find the freebie relevant to the usage pattern of the product being purchased, the promotional offer will hold no value in their minds.

Equally important is the value perception and here is another anecdote to illustrate this point. A detergent brand was offering a promotion involving gold coins to the shoppers. Shoppers purchasing the detergent had to drop in a coupon with their contact details and the winners would get a 1 gram gold coin every week in each of their stores. In addition, a grand monthly prize of a 5 gram gold coin was also on offer in every store. Although the offer was interesting and several shoppers participated in the same, the net result was not spectacular.

Based on my understanding of shopper-behaviour, my

suggestion to the team from the detergent manufacturer was to drop the gold coins and instead offer a small container with a lid. Although they were not very happy trading gold coins for plastic containers my credibility with regard to valid shopper insights convinced them. They agreed to try this alternative promotional offer of a free plastic container with every pack of detergent purchased.

To say that they were surprised or rather shocked by the incredible response is an understatement. They were amazed that the sales of that detergent zoomed and the increase was far more than what happened during the gold coin promotion. The insight which led to this was actually simple and is related to value perception in a shopper's mind.

There were two direct benefits that the plastic container delivered as compared to the gold coins. The first was the fact that everyone got something. It was not some kind of a contest where the chances of winning are always doubtful. I know many people, myself included, who never participate in any such contests simply because we have never won anything. As such that strong conditioning of our minds negates the value or worth of the prize in any contest. Even a high-end car, or an apartment or anything for the matter has zero value in the minds of such shoppers as they feel that they will not win that prize. Now, compared to a prize which they feel will never be theirs, a plastic container worth ₹10 has more value simply because ten is bigger than zero!

The second aspect which further reinforced the value of the freebie was its relevance. Every home pours the detergent into a container for daily use. Getting a good container along with the detergent was relevant and therefore of great value. Last, but not the least, there was a third aspect for this freebie to be effective, the utility of the product. Here again, the container scored over gold coins as every home always finds some use or the other for good plastic containers, especially in India.

Therefore, any freebie being given should fulfil these three aspects: relevance, value and utility.

Let me explain this in a different context before moving on. In the '90s, a well-known brand of potato chips started offering small, round pieces of plastic printed with bright colourful designs called Tazos. They were found inside every packet of chips and soon became a rage. Seen in isolation, this freebie made no sense whatsoever since it neither had relevance, utility nor any value. Yet, it became a rage among children and teens to such an extent that shoppers would buy packets of potato chips and consume it like there was no tomorrow. This craze led to instances of fights at schools and several schools even ended up banning Tazos. However, nothing affected this craze till the entry of video games when Tazos ended up making a quiet exit.

The actual rationale behind this craze and the success of that promotion was that Tazos did have relevance, offered utility albeit of a different kind and, therefore, had value in the minds of shoppers. In some cases, the small shop owners were known to open the packets in order to sell these Tazos at a higher price than the packet of chips themselves. This is a clear indication of the value that this freebie had in the minds of the shoppers.

Tazos became a cool thing to have and to collect. The collecting aspect led to the desire to amass these and soon a trend started where Tazos would be exchanged and bartered amongst children and teens. This tag of being a cool thing made it relevant to the shopper and the trend of collecting these and exchanging the same brought in an element of utility. Therefore, value was perceived and it is no wonder that this promotion became a runaway hit.

As a smart shopper, the only shift in mindset that is required is to evaluate the freebie independently without bringing in the aspect of it being relevant. This is because relevance can be very subjective as was gleaned from the example of the Tazos. As long as the freebie has utility, it will have value. In that context, the grocery items along with the television had great utility and therefore value if one were to remove the relevance aspect from the picture.

However, shoppers are not very fond of freebies for two important reasons. First is the practical reality that in many stores the free product is often not available, and the shopper needs to go back to pick up the same. Alternatively, the shopper is given something else as free which was not the key attraction in the first place and hence the core motivation to buy has been eroded.

The ideal choice to attract any kind of shopper is to give a simple straightforward discount. Shoppers also love this as it is easy to understand and they get the expected benefit without any hassle or delay.

However, various brands of products and organizations who manufacture these do not favour price discounts because it is considered to devalue the brand's worth in the shopper's mind. The rationale for this thinking is quite simple. Suppose a product is sold for ₹100 and frequently a discount of ₹10 is offered on it. In this case, shoppers would start to believe that the product is actually worth only ₹90. They would then wait for the discount to be offered to buy the product because for them, the perception about the worth of that product has changed. Although this is not a one-size-fits-all rule, this is broadly relevant and deters brands from discounting their products often. That is why you tend to see more of freebies being offered instead of a straightforward discount.

This shopper-behaviour of waiting for discounted prices is increasingly seen with regard to the various EOSS situations that are offered by lifestyle stores. It is becoming commonplace to see advertisements that offer up to 50 per cent or even up to 70 per cent off.

These promotional offers are usually available at lifestyle stores because they need to liquidate their stocks after a particular season. For example, the stocks in an apparel store during winter might be quite different from what they sell in summer. These stores offer such discounts in order to clear the unsold stock of products thereby freeing up the physical space in the store for fresh stock. They also bring in and prominently display a limited quantity of the new arrivals or stocks pertaining to the next season during such EOSS promotions. This ensures that while shoppers might come into the store drawn by the EOSS discount, they also see the new arrivals and, in many cases, end up buying some of that too.

However, oft-repeated and almost predictable EOSS offers have conditioned the shoppers to expect the sale regularly. This has led to a completely new sales trend where shoppers wait for such EOSS promotions and do their shopping only during this period. This new shopping behaviour has become so prevalent that many retailers now consider the EOSS periods as an additional sales opportunity and have started organizing extra stock to be sold during this period. From a retailer's perspective this is not a good trend, but, it is an excellent one from the point of view of a smart shopper.

Smart shoppers would typically plan and schedule their shopping during such periodic sale periods. The only downside to such shopping is that the products would typically be previous season's designs and styles. If that is not a priority for the kind of shopper you are, this is an excellent opportunity to shop. However, this would obviously not be valid for seasonal products like heaters or woollens. No shopper would like to buy a heater just when summer is around the corner. However, I also know of shoppers who stock up on such off-season products like woollen garments during EOSS promotions for the next winter!

What exactly happens in shoppers' minds that makes them respond to promotional offers and encourages them to rush to make that purchase?

Promotional offers basically leverage emotional responses through all the sensory elements discussed in the previous chapter along with the use of certain keywords in any retail communication.

The feelings which are predominantly triggered are a sense of urgency, a feeling of being special and being able to make smart choices. Let me explain each of these with an anecdote.

During the '90s when supermarkets were slowly making their way into the Indian shopping scene, the challenge was to bring shoppers into the store. This was largely because of the mindset discussed in the introduction about air-conditioned places being associated with expense. There was a specific promotion during every store launch called the 'Early Bird Special'. As the name suggests, this was only for shoppers who came early and the offer was a free 1.50 litre bottle of Coke worth ₹40 or so. The offer was applicable only for the first 50 or 100 customers who purchased for a minimum value.

The sheer number of shoppers who would line up for this offer from as early as 7.00 a.m. (for a store that opened at 9.00 a.m.) was mind-boggling. Over a period of time, we had to have queue managers to handle these early bird shoppers and this promotion slowly faded away as acceptance of supermarkets started to increase.

What motivated all these shoppers to get up early, get ready, come and stand in line for as long as two hours to get something worth ₹40 for free? This was clearly a sense of urgency triggered by the use of the term 'Early Bird' as it limited the number of shoppers who could avail this offer. The same feeling continues to be leveraged by retailers both in the physical store and online sites. The flash sales which are often advertised by online retailers are other examples of how a sense of urgency could be leveraged to make a shopper buy.

This urgency can also be triggered by creating a sense of scarcity. This was the effect when the early bird offer was limited to 50 or 100 customers. The same feeling of scarcity or rather the fear that one would lose out on a great deal is very real and has been proven through various retail studies. It has been repeatedly prove that when a product with promotion has a quantity restriction, it tends to sell more as compared to one with only a promotional offer. As an example, look at these two promotional offers in these two illustrations.

| XYZ | XYZ |
| :---: | :---: |
| **10%** OFF | **10%** OFF |
| | Only 5 units per bill |

A product has an offer of 10 per cent discount and the same product offers the same discount but there is a quantity restriction. The second offer would outsell the first one just because of the quantity restriction of 5 units per bill, in spite of all the other parameters being the same. In other words, a limitation on the quantity to be purchased creates a sense that the product is in short supply and hence the offer becomes more attractive as compared to one with only the discount. The word 'only' creates this sense of urgency that triggers purchase.

The other feeling which is successfully leveraged through promotions to influence shoppers is making them feel special. The fact is that we all love getting special treatment. It appeals to our sense of self-esteem and is a strong motivation for anyone. In a shopping context, this is done by highlighting something as a 'Special Offer of the Day' or offering a promotional offer to a select group of shoppers.

Many stores which have a loyalty programme successfully leverage this feeling by conducting a special sale. The EOSS is a frequent promotional scenario at several lifestyle stores and many of these retailers offer a special preview sale for the loyalty card members. The preview is usually held before the sale is open for everyone and only those with a loyalty card can avail the special sale prices. The retailer highlights this preview sale in order to make the loyalty card members feel special and induce them to come and do their shopping.

From the shopper's perspective, this feeling of being special is a trigger and it also induces a sense of urgency since the preview sale has a time limitation. Retailers use key words like special, exclusive, etc., to create this feeling and drive shopping.

The third feeling which triggers a shopper to buy is a sense of making a smart choice. You might have started to believe that shopping is a highly subconscious and irrational behaviour, based on what you have read till now. However, it is likely that you still believe that you are a smart, well-informed shopper. It would be very hard to accept that your shopping decisions are not smart and that thought is what is leveraged in some of the promotions.

You would often see promotions on soft drinks and juices which state: 'Buy 3 and Get 1 Free' or 'Take 4 and Pay for Only 3', etc. The message here is that you can take more than what you will be paying for. Most shoppers tend to pick up four packs of these juices or drinks even if they had planned to purchase only one or two, or maybe did not want to purchase them at all.

The conscious rationalization for such a purchase is that a product such as a juice or a soft drink would anyway get consumed and it is smarter to purchase them when there is such a good promotional offer. The perceived benefit is significant enough to influence the subconscious thought of making a smart choice by saving money.

However, the reality is that the shopper has ended up spending more than he or she planned by purchasing much more than what was required. Ironically, in the case of soft drinks or juices, such offers are given on stocks which are nearing the expiry date and the main objective is to clear them. So, the shopper has not only purchased more than what was required, but would have to consume that very soon or it would all go to waste.

This scenario is not limited to food-related purchases alone. I am confident that if you were to clean your storage space like your wardrobe or lofts, there would be a lot of such products which you purchased and have never used at all.

This same feeling of being special is also leveraged whenever a retailer offers you something at a special price if your bill value crosses a particular limit. If you recall the story I shared before about the woman in the Mercedes Benz who fought to get an extra plastic bucket, it was also based on the feeling of wanting to be special. She was not happy getting the same offer as everyone else and used her purchase value to fight for and get another plastic bucket. I would not be surprised if she had even forgotten about the plastic bucket by the time she reached home. The objective was not getting that bucket; the objective was to feel special.

There is a vegetable chopper which is usually sold in exhibitions and is nowadays also featured in the television shopping channels. It is actually a simple device and appears to be easy to use. I recall being very impressed by the salesman who would effortlessly peel, chop, slice and dice vegetables using this little contraption. Invariably, there would always be a crowd of eager shoppers wanting to buy this vegetable chopper once he finished his demonstration and I have also been one amongst them. However, once home, that device never lived up to my expectations and was finally thrown away in some corner. I often see many such devices and contraptions on the television shopping channels and you would be surprised to know that they sell very well. In fact, TV shopping is growing at a tremendous pace in India.

The key reason behind this growth and their sales is that they leverage all the three emotional aspects to influence shopping. It starts with showing a common problem like being fat or struggling to cut onions, etc. These are situations many people experience and can easily relate to. A simple solution is then shown with endorsements by others who have supposedly used this product and benefited. This establishes the authenticity of the solution and triggers the thought that making this purchase might be a smart thing to do.

Next is to offer a special price and in many cases a special gift which triggers the feeling of being special in your mind. Although, the rational mind might even consider the fact that the same offer is being made to millions of other viewers, your subconscious prefers to consider this as special for you. Finally the urgency is triggered by mentioning things like only for a limited period, call now, etc. I am not surprised by the growth rate of this retail channel and it might become bigger if the endorsements are presented in a better and more believable manner.

As a smart shopper, one should start by becoming aware of the emotional triggers which shape our responses towards promotions. Although there is nothing wrong in the emotional triggers that make a person feel special or smart, it is better to be cautious of the influence that such feelings can exert over shopping decisions. One of the fundamental, subconscious feelings which drive a shopper's response to promotions is the scarcity effect. Smart shoppers should always keep reminding themselves that this feeling of scarcity is more often than not a perception. It is not real.

Smart shoppers can further insulate themselves from the influences of promotional offers and their emotional triggers by consciously engaging in some rational thinking. For example, if you were to see an offer for any juices or soft drinks, check the manufacturing as well as the expiry date. Think if you can actually finish whatever you purchase before the expiry date. These conscious and factual thoughts might help you manage the emotional and impulsive ones.

A related activity to become a smart shopper would be to do frequent cleaning of your storage spaces at home. If you see anything which has not been used in the last one or two years, throw it away. However, before throwing it away, think back to when it was purchased and why you had bought the same. This would start creating a pattern about your shopping responses and if you understand that, managing such impulsive responses might become easier.

Last but not the least, always remember that the main objective of any promotion is to increase sales and liquidate stocks. That thought alone might help you become a smart shopper.

## KEY TAKEAWAY

- Promotions leverage the universal reality that everyone likes to get something for nothing.
- Any free offer would only be attractive if it is relevant to the purchase. In the shopper's mind, the free product has value and utility.
- The most attractive and also the simplest promotion is always a straightforward discount.
- Promotions always leverage one or more of these feelings—sense of urgency, feeling of being special, and being able to make smart choices.

## SMART SHOPPING HABITS

- Practice becoming aware of which feeling is getting triggered: urgency, feeling special or being smart.
- Consciously focus on some rational thinking when feeling any impulse or emotional response towards promotional offers.
- Check all the details of any product on promotion, especially the expiry date.
- Eat before going to a sale. Eating makes you feel satiated and you would be less likely to feel the scarcity urge.
- Shop with a list and try to stick to it. This would help you focus and shift your attention away from promotional offers.

# 6

# PESTER POWER

*The influence of children on shopping*

There is a very interesting and hilarious advertisement for a cold-related nasal congestion spray. The positioning of this product is that it would stop a cold if used at the first sign of anyone having one. Their sign-off line is that 'attack is the best form of defence'.

The advertisement starts with a woman in a store pushing a shopping trolley which has a toddler in it. She senses the start of a bout of cold because she coughs. She immediately pulls out the nasal spray, uses it and feels better. Meanwhile, her son has been pulling out things from another shelf and she looks at him to indicate that he needs to put the products back. He immediately throws the products on the floor and starts a tantrum. Then, the woman lies down on the floor and starts throwing a bigger tantrum. To say that the boy is shocked is an understatement. He stops his yelling and looks on at his mother who then gets up, looks at him with a look of nonchalance that clearly says that any tantrum you throw, I can better it by miles, nods at him to follow her and walks off. He realizes that his tantrum will not help. He puts the products back on the shelf and follows the woman. The voice in the background of the advertisement stresses the point that 'attack is the best form of defence'.

No description can do full justice to the way the models have acted in the advertisement. If you are curious and would like to see the advertisement, search online for 'nasal spray tantrum advertisement'. I am sure you will find this very interesting.

Obviously there are messages pertaining to parenting, indulging children in their whims beyond a point, etc., in this advertisement. There are and will always be debates and arguments about the correct parenting styles and the balance between being tough versus indulgent. This uncertainty of whether a person is being a good parent and is doing what is best for his/her children is leveraged extensively by marketers and advertisers. Every advertisement where a mother is worried about her child's health, height, teeth, or something else, plays on this guilt. Similarly every advertisement or marketing communication which questions the child's future education and its costs is again playing on this same emotional factor. Retailers also leverage a parent's mindset with regard to their children. Let me share some thoughts about that.

The reality is that when economies develop and the level of disposable incomes goes up, the mindset of people changes. As detailed in the introduction, the Gen X shoppers do operate with some remnants of the scarcity mindset which continues to influence their shopping. On the other hand, the Millennials have no such constraining influence as they are conditioned to expect things instantly. This expectation starts to set in early and is often allowed to remain as well as sometimes is also grown by the parents.

Two emotional factors drive the parents to indulge in their children's wishes and end up reinforcing the instant gratification orientation. The first is their own conflict of having grown up with scarcity and not having been able to fulfil their own indulgences during their growing up years. This leads to them having a very sympathetic view of the demands made by their children and they often give in to the same.

The other reason is a complex mix of emotions which leads to a feeling of guilt. The various factors which influence this guilt are all related to not being able to spend enough time with their children. Regardless of whether they are busy working or pursuing a lifestyle of their own choice, the result is that they feel that the children are not being given enough attention. This feeling is usually overcompensated by giving in to their demands through purchases and other materialistic options. Related to this is the self image of the younger parents who are themselves still in the instant gratification mode and feel compelled to cater to the same in their children.

Such conditioning creates a mindset which gives tremendous power to the child and is often misused by them. It manifests itself in the form of demands and if that is not met the child throws a tantrum, cries, shouts, etc. till the parent gives in.

Simply put this is what pester power is all about. Pester power is essentially the influence that children have over their parents' shopping behaviour. It could be something as simple as a hungry infant whose time for a feed is conflicting with shopping, or a young adult defining the technology product to be purchased, or a child demanding and throwing a tantrum about wanting something. From a retailer's perspective this influence can either help or hinder the shopping process and thus, it needs to be anticipated as well as managed. In many cases, the retailers understand the power that the children have over shopping and the fact that they influence their parents' shopping. The retailers leverage it to increase their sales. In few categories, this ends up interfering with shopping and if not managed properly, it might result in the loss of sales or at least a reduced sale value. Let me share some stories with examples to explain how retailers manage the various forms of pester power.

During a training programme I was conducting for a group of furniture store managers, the topic of pester power was being discussed. One of the participants shared an interesting experience and wanted some guidance from me regarding the same. The incident involved a young couple with a child who had come to the store to make purchases. They had relocated to the city recently and were planning on buying furniture for the entire house as they had decided against the hassle of shifting their old furniture. They went through the process of checking out the various options available for each of the rooms such as drawing room sofas, dining tables, beds and dressers for the bedroom, etc. Next steps in any furniture purchase is to shortlist the products and evaluate them in detail based on their features, colours, etc. Finally, the payment is discussed and the paperwork is done if the shopper decides to avail of the credit option. This is quite a time-consuming process and a child would obviously get very bored during this period.

As expected, the child who had accompanied the parents was initially curious and went around sitting on sofas, bouncing on the beds, opening the wardrobes, etc. However, there is only so much that can be explored by a child and soon boredom set in. He then went to his parents and announced that he was bored. The parents told him that they would finish soon and the store manager started to try and conclude their sale as she knew that the child getting bored was a dangerous sign. If the child started getting agitated and the sale had not been concluded the chances were high that it would not happen at all.

The child was quiet for a short while but then he demanded food as he was hungry. The parents again told him to wait saying that they were almost done. Soon the child came up with a demand which could not be put off; he wanted to go to the toilet. Thankfully for the store manager, the store had a toilet and could be used by the child. However, the basic issue of his boredom remained and it looked like the parents would abort the shopping because of the same.

The store manager was a quick thinker and led the child to her computer and opened a few games for him to play. This simple act kept the child occupied long enough for the sale to be completed. The question posed to me by the store manager was whether this was a common occurrence and what needs to be done by retailers to manage the same.

The best example I can give for handling such a situation is what IKEA does in their stores. IKEA is a Swedish multinational chain of stores which offers a wide range of ready-to-assemble furniture and other home-related products. Needless to say, these products would be of very little interest to any child and their boredom would influence IKEA sales. In most of the IKEA stores, they have a children's area which includes a play area, place to rest, eat, etc. In addition, they also offer a changing room for infants. Most importantly, they have a place to shop where products appealing to children and related to the home are displayed.

Simply put, they have managed to turn pester power to their advantage. Not only can parents shop freely and in a relaxed manner, but the children can also pick up some products and add to the sale. The IKEA store is a place where any child likes to go and that itself is a major benefit.

In the Indian context where the stores are not large enough to create such an area, retailers can and must do something different to keep the children engaged. One simple thing that can be done is to place stuffed toys in the children's furniture section. Apart from adding to the display to create a home like feeling, children can play with them and be engaged. Placing magazines or even a video gaming console in the area where sofas are displayed can keep older children engaged. This will become increasingly important as Millennials start their families and do their home-related shopping with their children. They would obviously prefer to go to a store where the children can be engaged while they shop.

As a smart shopper, if you want to shop for furniture or home-related products carry along something to keep the child engaged. Alternatively, if you want to keep your shopping short and contained, let the child become bored and that will act like an alarm clock to end your shopping.

Retailers whose range of product categories is interesting for children find that this task is easier to handle. They place such product categories at those heights where they can be early seen and accessed by children. All those chocolates and biscuits which are kept within easy reach of the children are there for a reason. Similar is the case of placing lot of impulse-driven products near the billing counters. Not only children but even adults who are waiting and becoming impatient would tend to get distracted by these products and end up buying the same.

The third and increasingly important influence of children on their parents' shopping is the decision of what to buy. Children today define the product category, brand choices, as well as the actual product to purchase. This influence often extends to the choice of retail outlet as well.

A friend of mine had to purchase a printer for his home and went to a consumer durables store. He had gone there with his family and while he was checking out the printers that were on display his daughter wandered off. She soon rushed back to ask permission for taking part in a colouring competition that the store had organized as an activity to keep the children engaged. It so happened that his daughter also won a prize for her entry. Needless to say, she now insists that all future electronic purchases should be done only from that store.

The opposite can also be true as seen in this story of another person I knew who was purchasing a mobile phone. He usually frequents a particular shop and the owner is known to my friend. When my friend's son wanted to purchase a new mobile, he was not very keen on going to the same shop. It could have been because of the imagery of that shop. However, my view is that this was strongly influenced by the fact that the owner would tend to focus on his parents as they were the main shoppers and perhaps ignore the son. As his father was insistent, he agreed to go to that shop and asked for the mobile in black. The shop did not have a black model and the owner tried to hard sell another colour saying that the black one was not available in the market. That single experience has been enough to ensure that the son will never ever purchase a mobile from that shop again. Not only that, his influence over the parents' shopping behaviour might lead to a shift in their choice of outlet as well.

This increasing influence of children over the parents' shopping choices is because of two important factors: more access to information and early adoption by younger shoppers.

Shopping is largely driven by the subconscious as I have already explained in varied scenarios. However, the actual thought process leading up to the decision involves a lot of rational thinking and making choices. In today's context where the shopper is confronted with multiple choices in terms of products, brands, features, retail options, etc., this leads to an overdose of information with regard to any purchase.

The younger generation is more comfortable with technology and indulges in higher usage of smartphones and the Internet. They are also active in a plethora of social media platforms and all of this gives them a lot of information. This abundance of information consists of multiple layers such as product and brand information, word of mouth as well as user feedback, comparisons, etc. All these tend to give the younger generation a better understanding of the shopping choices especially with regard to technology and lifestyle product categories. Therefore, it is but natural that their opinion gains credibility when it comes to shopping, especially in these categories.

The younger consumers are usually early adopters of any new product, technology or service. This means that they are more open to try new things and explore alternatives. As such these shoppers would be better informed about new products, trends, etc.

These are the two main reasons why children are increasingly becoming active participants in the decision-making process for purchases, especially when it comes to technology or lifestyle product categories. The flip side to this behavioural trend is that children get habituated to having a say in the purchases being made regardless of whether they know anything about them or not. This tends to create situations where the child wants to take on the decision-making role instead of only participating in the thinking process.

The last dimension of pester power relates to the access to money and finances of the parents. It is quite common to see children getting pocket money to spend. In addition, they might also have an add-on credit card. I have also noticed children who have a free access to their parents' credit card and use that for making online purchases where a physical cheque is not required.

This behavioural trend reinforces their faith and confidence that they can make purchases independently which is both good and bad. It is good for obvious reasons that this confidence would help them in growing up without insecurities. The flip side is the delinking between spending and earning that happens because of such behaviour. Such shoppers tend to spend, especially using their credit cards, to an extent where the expenses are far higher than the income levels. Such behaviour, driven by lifestyle and coupled with various other points mentioned earlier, puts enormous pressure on the parents.

As smart shoppers, one must first become aware and accept that pester power is real and it exists. Just like how retailers leverage pester power, shoppers can do it too. It should start with being very firm with children about shopping. Although, indulging one's children is fine, repeatedly doing so especially while shopping, creates a behavioural pattern which would become hard to break.

One of the biggest pitfalls that parents should avoid is the trap of what others would think. In that context, I would strongly urge you to watch the video I have mentioned at the start of this chapter. If that mother had been apprehensive of what others would think, she might not have gained control over the situation so easily. On the other hand, children, especially smaller ones, do not have this concern. Children are rarely bothered about the reactions and opinions of strangers. That is what enables them to cry, shout, roll on the floor in a public place and get their way. They are in no hurry to stop while the parent is pressurized to make the child stop misbehaving. The easier option that parents tend to choose is to give in to the child in order to put an end to the tantrum.

As mentioned before, take the children along for boring categories like furniture if you want an alarm check to curb your shopping. Alternatively, don't take the children along if you want to indulge in leisurely shopping, as not all stores would have enough options to engage a child.

An important practice to manage pester power and cultivate a habit of smart shopping in children is by delegating the shopping process as well as offering a reward.

I know of families where children are given a part of the shopping list. Then, as a reward they are allowed to pick up anything worth a certain value. The breakup of the list and the limit on the reward are set before going to the store and there is no room for any discussion at the store. You would be surprised at the results. Children learn to choose what they want as the reward and they also learn that they cannot demand everything that catches their fancy. Involving them in this activity also helps to break down any gender bias and establishes that it is to be done by everyone. Last and definitely not the least, the parents are not stressed out after every shopping trip. If you have children, do try it.

## KEY TAKEAWAY

- Pester power is the influence children have on their parents' shopping behaviour.
- Retailers are aware of pester power and try to counter the same or leverage its power.
- The inputs of Millennials and the younger generation of shoppers play a big role in the shopping decisions of few product categories.
- Children are oblivious to the reaction of strangers which gives them the freedom to behave in whichever way they want. Parents are often not firm enough because they are concerned about what others would think.

## SMART SHOPPING HABITS

- Take children along for product categories which might not be of interest to them and therefore they will curtail your shopping.
- Cultivate the habit of smart shopping in children by making them take ownership and responsibility with regard to money.
- Involve them in shopping by giving them a list and make them shop for those items.
- Give them some amount of money to purchase what they wish while shopping. This amount should not be increased without any valid reason.
- Never feel awkward about disciplining children who are not behaving properly while shopping.

# 7

# I WANT IT NOW!

*Online and mobile-driven shopping and shopping behaviour*

A few decades ago if one were to travel by air the passenger would be given a physical ticket which would consist of a few pages and was almost like a small booklet. Some of the readers might have used such tickets and a few others might have even seen it. This practice of issuing tickets in physical form has died and today a passenger prints their one page ticket or in many cases just prints the boarding pass. A lot of passengers don't even do that and show the ticket on their mobile and enter the airport. The next step would be to only show the boarding pass on the mobile and anything in a printed, physical form would have completely disappeared.

Is online the future for retail as well? Will physical stores make way for online shopping? Will shoppers even come to physical stores? How can physical stores compete? Why do shoppers purchase from online sites? Why should they continue to come to physical stores?

These form the a barrage of questions that are directed to me at almost every forum, be it a training programme, workshop, conference or even a consulting assignment. Although I do understand the underlying sense of unease about handling change and its implications, I personally think that the online shopping aspect is being blown out of proportion. This is largely due to the disproportionate share of coverage in media which often has big headlines about millions of dollars being given as funding.

Let us go back to the basics that define and drive online transactions to understand more about online shopping and all the related aspects. Online transactions were largely pioneered by airlines, travel and hospitality services. The feeling of apprehension as well as concerns related to sharing credit card details online was amongst the first few barriers to online transactions. This has slowly changed over the years. Another major worry in the minds of many customers was that whether they would actually get the benefits from the products or service being paid by them. The immediate issue of an online ticket went a long way in allaying this concern and spurring the trend of online purchases.

From the perspective of airlines the trend of online bookings represented a major shift in their distribution costs. They no longer had to pay travel agents to book and issue tickets. The costs of the printed booklets for a ticket could be avoided and that in itself was a major saving. The cost of operating the flights was separate and not linked to the process of booking the tickets.

This essentially is the most important and basic difference between online travel bookings as compared to online shopping. In the case of online shopping, the cost of distribution is core to the business of any retailer. In online shopping, the actual receipt of goods by the shopper needs to be fulfilled in a very different manner.

The initial catalyst for online retail was that these businesses would be more profitable as there would be no need to open physical stores and pay high rentals for the same. However, the real estate costs have been substituted by delivery costs of making the products reach the shopper's home. As such this transaction is very different from that of online travel-related transactions.

Where businesses like airlines actually saved money by moving to an online booking platform, online retailers have only traded the cost of real estate for delivery costs. This is a challenge which is becoming tough to manage.

The common element across all online transactions pertains to convenience. Especially when Internet access is becoming faster, better, and available across various devices, this aspect of convenience is assuming a larger role in the minds of shoppers. The changing urban landscape which has led to increased commuting time along with traffic woes have added up to create the perception of convenience while shopping online.

However, convenience alone is not enough to change shopping behaviour and several other concerns need to be addressed before a wholehearted shift happens in the shopper's mind. Similar to some of the initiatives that supermarkets and other modern self-service stores took in the '90s, online retailers are doing things to create a shift in the buying behaviour.

One of the earliest advertisements for a major Indian online retailer showed a couple watching a cricket match and betting on the outcome of the next ball of the over. The winner would then immediately place an order for the product they had selected. The first thought when I saw the advertisement was about how the couple will manage to pay for all these purchases. That was a classic Gen X response! When I started thinking about the same after wearing my retailer and shopper-behaviour hats, some interesting aspects of the advertisement became evident. Also, how it would influence the viewers became obvious.

This advertisement showed a couple with no children. There is even a term used by marketers for such consumers:

DINKS—Double Income No Kids. Such consumers could be Gen Xers or even Millennials. They obviously have a higher level of disposable income which they tend to spend on lifestyle purchases. This aspect was highlighted by the choice of the products being selected for the bet. The male was looking to buy a gaming console while the woman was betting for bags, shoes, etc. They had a laptop in front of them and would click the buy button after every ball which communicated the ease of the actual purchase. Last was the obvious message where the large number of products available was highlighted.

The message was clearly targeted at that group of shoppers who would be open to experimentation and adoption of newer things like online shopping and also would have the money to spend.

Similarly, the first campaign of the competing online site showed small children dressed like adults and speaking like them. The conversations would typically revolve around the ease of shopping, etc. This again had a sublime message aimed at the Millennials while also leveraging the unsaid message of how online shopping is easy and convenient enough for even children to do so.

Although such messages are good enough to influence perception and create imagery in the minds of shoppers, it takes much more to make shoppers break their existing habit and shift to online shopping. Even the Millennials who are faster to adopt new things, do take time to change their habitual behaviour and need a strong enough stimulus to do the same.

As already discussed, shopping habit is built on trust and breaking the trust factor and making a shopper shift to another store or site requires that he or she starts to at least consider trusting the alternative site or store. This is a catch-22 situation in shopping. Trust is built on experience of the shoppers and a new store or site cannot establish this trust unless the shopping happens with them. Ironically, shoppers will not come and purchase unless they trust the store or site.

Massive discount sales at unbelievable prices helps trigger such a trial which might lead to trust and, therefore, a shift in the shopping behaviour. Most of these massive discounts are for limited periods and are also available on limited quantity. This triggers the scarcity feeling in shoppers by creating a sense of urgency. Also, they want to be special by being able to get that product at an unbelievable price.

I know of several Millennial shoppers who purchased thumb drives in such sales at ₹1 only to be able to say that they got that product at such a low price. Interestingly, this is not something new and was done by Deccan Air when they came into the market decades ago. This technique is often used by low-cost carriers even today. These initiatives helped to create a new shopper base that had tried out these online sites and were now open to continuing their shopping through these sites. These shoppers were largely Millennials as the whole online buying behaviour fits in well with their orientation of ease, convenience and quick.

On the other hand, Gen X shoppers did try online sites in a limited manner and came away with mixed feelings. They appreciated the value they got from low prices but the instances of bricks being delivered instead of phones, delay in delivery, etc., ended up reinforcing their doubts about online shopping.

This led to another round of advertising and messaging which addressed these concerns by talking about genuine products, easy returns and exchanges, etc.

Advertisements to address the concerns pertaining to returns and exchange by two leading online shopping sites have an interesting exchange between two people. In both the advertisements, the exchange is between a Millennial and a Gen X shopper where the younger shopper is seen as endorsing online shopping in terms of the ease of returning products while the older shoppers appear doubtful about the same. In one of the advertisements, the older shopper says that he could convince his regular shop owner to exchange the sari, if required. To this the younger shopper says that he does not need to convince anyone and can easily exchange or return anything on the online site.

It is clear that the efforts of online retailers are targeted at breaking the existing shopping habits and inducing a shift to online shopping. Another development in this context is the advent of mobile apps which every online retailer promotes. The focus on mobile apps is so intense that a site actually allowed shopping only through their app. However, over a period of time, they reversed this stand as it obviously did not go down very well with shoppers. Increasingly, physical store chains are also introducing online sites for shopping to leverage the preference of online purchases by a segment of shopper.

This brings me to the question about the future of retail and whether online sites would replace physical stores.

Online shopping will definitely be a part of the choices available to shoppers. It will continue to cater to a specific set of shoppers as well as dominate a few product categories. However, physical stores would also continue to exist as shoppers do give importance to the 'Touch, Feel and See' aspect of shopping. This could very well be the reason why Amazon, which is considered to be one of the biggest names in online shopping, recently moved into the physical store space. They have opened a physical bookstore in the USA to the surprise of many people.

Online shopping caters to the shopping behaviour of Millennials and it will gain prominence as they become older and their shopping basket expands. Current trends and the sales figures of online retailers support this hypothesis and clearly indicate a strong bend towards the Millennials possessing the ideal shopper profile. In addition, online shopping is dominated by sales of mobiles, mobile accessories and lifestyle products such as clothing. This is yet again indicative of shoppers who have a higher level of disposable income and who are not shopping for functional reasons.

Apart from offering a wide range of choices, the ease and convenience of shopping is a major factor which appeals to the Millennials and also some of the Gen X shoppers. The move towards online shopping by Gen Xers is also increasingly being influenced by their children's shopping experiences and is yet another example of how the children exercise influence over their parents' shopping behaviour.

One of the biggest advantages that online shopping has over physical stores is the capability to customize and personalize the shopping process for each customer. Physical stores have been trying to do this for many years now and they often use a loyalty card as a tool to do this. Although the shoppers usually associate any loyalty card with reward points and special offers, the retailer is spending on it for one reason only: to obtain information and data about shopping patterns and behaviours.

Whenever a shopper is using their loyalty card to get points, they are also identifying that transaction and all the details regarding the same for the retailer. The retailer, over a period of time, builds up data about how often you shop, what you buy, when you buy it, etc. This information is used to plan for special offers which will be attractive to an individual or at least a similar group of shoppers and motivate them to buy. This data and information is analysed using the extensive information technology options and software available nowadays which not only create a profile of the shopper but even predict the behaviour of a shopper.

If you think that this sound like a science-fiction fantasy, you are completely wrong. This is as real as it can get.

A leading American supermarket chain had done exactly this kind of data analysis and discovered a pattern. They found that when women shoppers were following a particular pattern in terms of buying certain products, it often indicated that they were pregnant. Based on this information, they started to send special promotional coupons for baby products, maternity clothing, etc.

A customer came into one of their stores one day and had a showdown with the store manager because his teenage daughter had received such a letter with coupons. The manager promised to look into this and before he could do anything that customer called him with an update.

The customer very sheepishly told the manager that his daughter was indeed pregnant and that he had been unaware of certain developments at his home. Imagine that, the retailer knows that a person is pregnant before her family gets to know.

The only catch in this kind of analysis is the dependence on a shopper's willingness to show their loyalty card and identify any purchase as being made by him. If that teenager had not flashed her loyalty card and identified the purchase as being made by her, she would have never got the letter. That is always an option for any shopper if they wish to protect their privacy with regard to their shopping.

However, the online shoppers today are constantly sharing a similar identification tag which links everything they do. This identification tag is your mobile number and in a lot of cases the credit card details also.

Every online shopper ends up sharing these details for every transaction and thereby identifies every transaction they made online. The increasing trend of using mobile phone apps for online purchases is making it even easier for getting all these data and information. That is the main rationale why online retailers promote the usage of their apps so aggressively. Of course the other reason for promoting the use of apps is to lock in the shopper in terms of preferences. After all a shopper would tend to make purchases from existing apps installed on their phone and which they are comfortable using instead of downloading new ones. These mobile apps often are active all the time and might even collect information that is not about any online purchases.

A whole new business and industry has grown out of the collection and analysis of this kind of data and information. It is known as analytics, and it relies very heavily on Big Data.

Big Data is the collection and collation of information about an individual or groups from varied and also independent data sources. Big Data and analytics is what enables any site to show advertisements which are relevant and will appeal to you when you browse. The extent of the amount of information and the capability of such data to know about a person and predict their behaviour is obvious from a simple fact that Facebook seems to know a person as well as their spouse!

In 2015, a study was done by the University of Cambridge and Stanford University which involved 86,000 Facebook users. They asked the users themselves as well as their friends and family to complete a personality questionnaire. This was compared to an analysis done of the 'Likes' they had clicked on, on the various posts to predict their personality. The results were shocking and clearly Facebook seemed to know the users better than anyone else.

This vast data and the capability to analyse and predict human behaviour is being put to use by Amazon, the online shopping giant. Amazon has got a patent for this algorithm-based approach which is supposed to predict what a shopper will purchase. Details of this system are not very clear for obvious reasons related with competitive advantage. However, at a broad level this algorithm would track all the previous purchases and as soon as a shopper starts browsing it will predict the purchases of the shopper. Amazon would then have that product picked up and kept ready to be sent to the customer once they actually complete the order. The beauty of this system is that it would learn from every mistake made in the prediction and keep correcting the predictive process.

From a shopper's point of view this is fantastic as the delivery time gets cut down and they would get the products faster. The convenience factor of online shopping gets reinforced if their orders get delivered at the earliest. The same convenience factor is leveraged to encourage shoppers to remain logged into the site, save their credit card details, etc. All the while such shopping and online behaviour keeps on generating mountain loads of data about the shopper.

The older generation of shoppers would be extremely uncomfortable with this as privacy and the related security issues are very dominant in their minds. Gen X shoppers are relatively more accepting about sharing information about themselves and trading off their privacy for other benefits. Millennials on the other hand have a very different approach to sharing information about themselves online.

They realize that there is enough information about everyone already freely available online. They also know that they add to it through their various social media posts as well. Every post, picture, video, like and share creates a better understanding about that person. The Millennials are already aggressive social media users, especially through their smartphones. In most cases, they are not even aware about the extent of data they are sharing and in many cases they do not care even if they know.

Their priority with regard to shopping is convenience, speed of fulfilment and getting the latest range. If any retailer caters to this, data being shared is a trade off they are willing to accept. In that context, online retailers are increasingly focusing their efforts on catering to this group of shoppers especially their core expectation of instant gratification.

This expectation of instant gratification is leading to a new form of retailing called as Omni Channel retail. Although this is still a very nebulous idea and there are widely differing definitions and perspectives as to what constitutes Omni Channel, the common thread is that this should offer a seamless shopping experience across physical and online shopping options.

A term which is emerging with regard to Omni Channel is—BAFARA. It stands for 'Buy Anywhere, Fulfil Anywhere and Return Anywhere'.

Suppose you are returning from office and need to pick up some products as guests are expected at home. You realize that you do not have enough time to stop and complete your shopping and yet you require snacks, some other food items, soft drinks, etc. With the help of BAFARA, the shopper would be able to go to the app of the retailer and place an order for the required items as well as select the delivery option. You could also choose to pick up your shopping from a store on your way. Since you would have already made the payment through your mobile, all that would be required would be to dash into the store, pick up the bags and keep moving. It could even be possible that there is a separate take away counter like a pizza outlet where you could pick up the products without even going into the store. Additionally, if on reaching your home, you realize that you had ordered something which you cannot use or do not require, you could use the app to place a return request and specify a time to have the unwanted product collected from your home or office.

BAFARA, essentially, means scenarios like this where the shopper can transact across various channels like online and physical stores. At a conceptual level it sounds fantastic and also doable. However, there are several practical constraints which would take time to resolve before true BAFARA becomes a mainstream reality.

From a shopper's perspective, such convenience comes at a cost of being locked in with retailers because a retailer would prefer to offer this kind of service and convenience only to regular, loyal shoppers. Every retail outlet starting from the neighbourhood small stores attempts to potray that they will go the extra mile for their shoppers. However, the unsaid caveat is that this is usually done for the regular and loyal shoppers only.

I stayed alone in Bengaluru for a while and there was the ubiquitous kirana store near my apartment complex. Once I moved in, I went and introduced myself and was promptly given the telephone number of the store owner along with an invitation that I can call anytime for anything. I was also reassured that it would be sent immediately. Since I used to travel very frequently, I did not purchase very often from that store. The few times I did stop there, I purchased one or two products. Thus, it was clear that I was neither a regular nor a high-value customer. A few months later, I called the shop to send across some soft drinks and packed snacks as I had guests. The shop owner was apologetic but firmly said that he could not send it across as his delivery boy was not available. Left with no other option, I went down to purchase these items and bumped into the delivery boy who was entering the compound with some things to deliver, but they were obviously not for me.

Clearly the shop owner did not feel that my patronage deserved prompt delivery. Similar is the case of any extent of service. If retailers move towards BAFARA as a standard, the qualifier would be regular and frequent shopping. In other words, the retailer would try to lock-in your shopping choice as far as possible in exchange for value-added elements like convenience.

However, this lock-in is already happening with regard to online and mobile shopping. This would become even more habitual if Omni Channel comes into the picture in a true sense of offering BAFARA. One of the costs for such convenience would definitely be compromising one's privacy. However, this might soon become a non-issue because of the online behaviour of people, especially the Millennials. In the trade off for convenience, they knowingly or unknowingly already leave enough bread crumbs of data about themselves.

A simple example is the use of location-tracking feature on mobile phones which is mandatory if you are using any app-based cab service. Even otherwise users are increasingly keeping their location-tracking feature switched on. There are both pros and cons to this. The advantages of this range from simple indulgence of checking into places and receiving special offers because of the same to the important benefit of safety where any safety app can track your mobile all the while.

The flip side is that a person is clearly sharing enough information online with regard to where they go, when they go there and if any mobile-based transactions are done, it also gets linked to that particular location. These kinds of information are what are enabling sites to know you better than maybe even yourself!

Clearly the emerging value definition in the minds of shoppers is skewed towards experience and convenience. Price is an important aspect but the shoppers would slowly tend to believe that they are getting the best deal taking into account all that they are getting. This would be very similar to the scenario mentioned earlier where housewives believed that they were getting the best quality and price for the rice they purchased simply because that is what they chose to believe.

This trend is clear from the instance of Amazon developing predictive-picking algorithm as mentioned earlier in the chapter. A similar convenience factor that Amazon offers in the US is called the Amazon Dash Button. It is a small button which is paired with the Amazon app through WiFi and is usually linked to a particular brand. These buttons can be stuck on any surface or hung using the hook built into the device.

Suppose you have purchased the Dash button for a detergent that you normally use. Then, this button would be stuck on to the washing machine at your home. When you notice that the quantity of detergent is low, all you have to do is press that button. It would automatically trigger an order for that detergent which would then get delivered. If you searched for Amazon Dash Button on their dot com site, you would be amazed at the range of brands for which these devices are now being sold. This device and the related service are for their Amazon Prime customers only. Amazon Prime is a programme where customers sign up for a preferential set of services and value adds by paying a fee. These value adds could include free eBook downloads of several titles as well as the Amazon Dash facility.

So, clearly the shoppers are ready to pay and also share their information freely in exchange for convenience and other value added services. This trend is bound to pick up pace in India too as the number of Millennials and younger shoppers grow and become a large chunk of Indian shoppers.

Soon, technology would start to play an increasingly large role in redefining the shopper-behaviour. Technology is developing at a rapid pace and there are two particular developments which might redefine shopping experience as we know it today. One such technology is the rapid advance in 3D printing which is reaching a point where it will become affordable and mainstream. That day is not far when homes start having a 3D printer along with their home printers.

Three-dimensional printers, as the name suggests, can print or rather create 3D objects. Today, this technology has been successfully used to print a wide and diverse range of things such as 3D printed pizzas, 3D printed lockets and even 3D printed tissues. A while ago a person in America used this technology to print a plastic gun and fire real bullets.

The actual working of 3D printers is somewhat similar to a typical inkjet printer. While in an inkjet printer, ink is used, in a 3D printer, composite materials, plastic, etc. are used. The printer keeps layering the material one on top of the other as per a 3D diagram till the product has been created. The only constraint in this technology is that these devices are not very affordable and thus have not been adopted in large numbers by the public.

Once the prices of such a device become affordable and there are 3D drawings for products available online, a shopper might very well purchase the 3D drawing and print out the product at their home. For example, you go out with your friends and happen to see a stylish pair of footwear or a bag which you want to purchase immediately. It could very well become possible that you can browse and purchase the 3D drawing for that product and send it to your 3D printer at home for it to get printed. The product is ready and waiting for you by the time you reach home.

Obviously there are other constraints such as materials for different products might have to be loaded separately on to the printer, the product might get printed in pieces and would have to be assembled later, etc. However, these might also be overcome using technology over a period of time.

The other technology which might have a far-reaching impact on shopping is Mixed Reality as well as Virtual Reality (VR). Virtual Reality is creating a computer-generated simulation of 3D objects or environment where the user can interact with the same using special equipment. Mixed Reality is when the VR simulation integrates with the existing real world and physical surroundings.

Virtual Reality is more about watching lifelike simulations whereas Mixed Reality would enable the user to have a higher level of interaction with the simulation. Microsoft is working on a product named HoloLens. As per their official site, 'Microsoft HoloLens is the first fully self-contained, holographic computer, enabling you to interact with high-definition holograms in your world'.

Such technology would enable a shopper to do more realistic online shopping than ever before. While online shopper today looks at a flat screen, these technologies might bring the online sites to life and project them in front of the shoppers. The detailing possible in such a scenario is mind-boggling and shoppers could even customize the store to their tastes and preferences. Such developments are still in the future but one never knows how soon the future will arrive.

This is especially true for Indian shoppers who are only

now experiencing and slowly getting habituated to online and mobile shopping. If Virtual Reality and Mixed Reality are adopted by retailers, shoppers might jump straight onto this platform instead of using the passive screen-based online shopping.

Imagine a scenario where you come home and relax on your recliner, wear your Virtual Reality or Mixed Reality device and bring your favourite store to life. You can window shop, browse, and purchase all from the comfort of your recliner. Which shopper would not like this, especially if they consider convenience as a very important factor?

So, the actual 'Touch, Feel and See' experience might be replaced with only 'Feel and See', but you never know, technology might even come up with a solution to duplicate the real life 'Touch, Feel and See' experience. Shoppers might no longer go to stores but stores would come to their homes in every which way they want them.

In case you think that all these futuristic space-age scenarios are far-fetched, this is actually closer to reality than we think. Let me share some recent developments which clearly show that the future of shopping might be very different from what we have experienced till now.

Shoppers can purchase 3D printers and customized products online from sites such as Shapeways, i.materialise, thingify, etc. Amazon has taken this to the next level and its further plans include a patented 3D printing truck which would come to your doorstep and print out the product. When 3D printers become affordable and mainstream, you could do the same at home. Another dimension of making your own product is printing your own copy of a book. A store in France uses an Espresso Book Machine which prints, cuts and binds a book right in front of your eyes. All this is completed in the time taken for the shopper to have a cup of coffee.

A realistic Virtual Reality shopping which might even use holographic projections to make it totally immersive is not far away. eBay, Australia is trying out a Virtual Reality shopping experience for their customers in association with Myers, a leading departmental store chain in Australia. Very clearly the way we perceive shopping is going to undergo a paradigm shift and so will shopper-behaviour.

Clearly some exciting times are ahead for shoppers and newer shopping experiences are expected to influence them in multiple ways. These developments would be aligned to the shopper expectations of Millennials, other future generations as well as some of the Gen X shoppers. Both men and women might adopt these new shopping paradigms with equal enthusiasm although it would be for very different product categories in the case of each gender.

Regardless of all these developments and in the current context of online and mobile shopping, what can a smart shopper do?

Smart shoppers must realize that online shopping leverages key aspects of their behaviour. The impulse-driven desire to purchase is facilitated by the convenience of completing that transaction. Very simply put, smart shoppers should counter these factors. Avoid online or mobile browsing of shopping sites especially if you are bored or feeling dull. Keep in mind the Dopamine influence. Browsing is like window shopping and the transaction is only one step away.

Even if you are browsing and cannot help it, make the

completion of the transaction slightly difficult. This can be done by not storing your credit card details on the site or the app. Chances are that if you get up to fetch your card for details, you might end up reconsidering the purchase unless it is actually required. Another little trick would be to use a particular card for online transactions and keeping this card locked up in your wardrobe. The ritual of opening the wardrobe and getting the card out might again give you some time to overcome the impulse to purchase.

Having a separate credit card, especially with a low credit limit would also act as a check on impulse buying. More importantly, if the card is lost or the details are stolen, the overall financial risk would be limited in scope.

Smart shoppers, especially in India, would also know that online retailers give unbelievable discounts to establish this habit of online shopping. As such, it might be judicious to take advantage of these fabulous, low prices while it lasts because it would not last forever. Although discounts would always be a part of online shopping, ridiculously low prices might not last for long.

Smart shoppers should be prudent and take the trouble to read the various details as well as the terms and conditions when making any online purchase. This is very important in the context of confirming important details such as the model, colour choice, terms of delivery, etc. Smart shoppers should also take the trouble to compare across shopping sites even if they prefer and are habituated to one store. This comparison should also extend to physical stores, in case of certain high-value product categories.

There is a debate about the role of cookies in our computers and smartphones. These small files are stored by the sites in order to make it easier for them to customize their content. However, this customization can work against the shopper also. A debatable practice when booking airline tickets is to clear the cookies and the computer cache before opening the travel or airline site. This is supposed to clear out any past record of your search and the site might show you a very low price. Several frequent travellers have shared that they have got much lower prices from the same site after they deleted the cookies and cleared the cache. This is debatable as these sites deny that their cookies influence the prices being displayed and that the prices are subject to demand and supply.

However, cookies do play their part in tracking what you do and the best example would be if you searched for something and then when you log into your online email account or social media, you start to see advertisements for that product or similar products. Smart shoppers regularly clear their cache and delete the cookies on their computer and smartphones.

If you are particular about your privacy and would not like to trade that for convenience, follow some of the safe browsing practices. Use the online site instead of the app, remember to clear cookies before opening the online shopping site, and disable the location-tracking feature unless you keep it on for the sake of security. Last but not the least, avoid saving your financial details on either the site or the app.

A smart shopper should always keep in mind what they are trading in return for the 'I want it now' orientation and be prepared for the implications.

**KEY TAKEAWAY**

> Online shopping is here to stay. However, physical stores are also not going anywhere.
> Convenience is the key trigger for online shopping. Subsequent factors like range of products and discounts are added attractions for shoppers.
> Online shopping fulfils the Millennial shopper's expectations of convenience, instant gratification, and availability of latest and trendy products.
> Gen X shoppers are also slowly warming up to online shopping because of the convenience factor as well as the fact that they have started to trust this shopping option.
> Shoppers are increasingly sharing information and data about themselves and their shopping behaviour in an extensive manner.
> BAFARA is a key shopper expectation which is what Omni Channel is trying to cater to.
> Technology will influence shopping and shopper-behaviour to a large extent in the coming years.
> Virtual Reality and Mixed Reality might soon bring the store to your home.

**SMART SHOPPING HABITS**

> Be aware and careful about the extent of information being shared online.
> Try to shop online using the computer instead of the app, and log in and log out every time. Every additional

> activity or work you do will help to manage impulsive shopping.
> - Avoid saving and storing your credit card details on any online shopping site.
> - Have a separate credit card with a lower credit limit.
> - Clear the cookies and the cache on your computer and smartphone regularly.

# 8

# DO SHOPPERS KNOW HOW TO GET GOOD SERVICE?

*Customer service and why getting good service is difficult*

The much maligned image of Air India, our national airline, is well known. The service crew in the aircraft is often the butt of jokes and majority of passengers do not consider them as providers of good service. This is one side of the scenario. Once I happened to interact with few stewards and stewardesses from the airline and posed this question to them as to why they are perceived to be unhelpful, unfriendly, and sometimes downright rude. Also, why does this attitude seem to be directed at Indian fliers while foreigners get a smile?

The response left me thinking as it was something I could empathize with having seen similar situations in various stores.

Their response was to share a typical scenario in the aircraft as the passengers would start to come in. The passengers would first of all ignore their wishes and smile and brush past them near the entrance. Once inside the aircraft, many of the passengers would try to literally stuff their grossly overloaded hand baggages into the overhead compartment. In many cases, a passenger might call the staff member and demand that they keep the bag on top. The flight ahead would be full of demands and in many cases rude, dismissive behaviour. On the other hand, most foreigners tended to wish these crew members when wished, they would request instead of demanding, and use words like please and thank you, etc.

The gist of the response is that Indian fliers, first of all, do not believe in acknowledging any wishes. Second, they are rude and do not know how to politely request for help; instead they tend to order the crew members around. Not only that, the passengers would invariably be aggressively demanding as well as rude.

It could very well be that there are exceptions to both Indian and foreign travellers who behave differently. However, this is the perception that these staff members have which must be due to the fact that the majority behaves like this.

I am inclined to believe their perspective because I have seen similar rude, demanding, aggressive and sometimes obnoxious behaviour by shoppers in several stores, repeatedly.

The reality is that most of the retail staff members are trained to smile, wish and offer help. To be fair to them, the majority start off their retail careers trying their best to do this. However, most of these customer service staff members tend to stop doing this. First, they stop the smiling bit, then they stop wishing, and finally they do not offer to help. This degeneration of service behaviour is to such an extent that the members start to ignore the customers unless called for specifically.

To give you a perspective of their reality I would suggest that you smile and wish people without fail for a whole day and then reflect on the experience.

I am sure that first of all you will feel fatigued by the effort of having to smile for such a long period of time. However, even that might not be an issue. More importantly, you will definitely feel very irritated when someone ignores you or gives a blank stare in return.

In my earlier book, *Break Free,* I have suggested the same exercise in order to understand the impact of emotions and body language on one's communication. Although smiling at known people tends to elicit a smile in return and helps to establish a rapport which helps in communication, such a response is very rare in any service situation. Consider the last time you had called a customer service number and think back if you wished the person in return when they wished you. If you had done so then you are an exception to the rule.

You might relate to the situation faced by the service staff whether in an airline or a retail store. From the perspective of the staff, it is not a pleasant experience and it is no wonder that they stop smiling, wishing, etc.

My observation of shoppers interacting with service staff whether in person or over the phone has led me to believe that the majority do not know how to get good service. In many instances, I have observed shoppers who do not deserve any service, leave alone good or bad.

Let me explain why many people do not know how to get good service with an example.

I was flying out to conduct a training programme about service, had completed the formalities at the airport and was waiting at the boarding gate. After a while, it became obvious that the flight was going to be delayed since there was no sign of any announcement about the beginning of the boarding process. As expected, a staff came and announced a delay due to technical reasons while the same was also being said over the public address system.

The passengers crowded around him and wanted various details about the delay. Someone had a connecting flight, another person wanted to cancel his booking as he could not attend a meeting, etc. I was trying to get a clearer picture in order to take a decision and was enquiring as to the nature of the technical problem and what kind of solution was being tried. It so appeared that one of the propellers of the aircraft was not starting properly and the engineering team had repaired the same. They were conducting tests to ensure that the issue had been completely resolved.

While this conversation was happening another passenger started shouting at the staff and her angst was that she had been delayed by a few minutes yesterday and therefore missed her flight. She had been put on the next day's flight and that was rankling her. Her stand was that she could not enter the airport yesterday since her mobile was not connecting to the net, hence, she could not show the ticket to the security which caused her delay. Her contention was that she had also faced technical problems and yet had to miss the flight whereas she was now being delayed due to technical problems being faced by the airlines.

It took some time for the staff to even understand her issue since she kept referring to her technical problem which had caused her delay. Even after understanding the issue, the staff member was not in any position to help as her issue did not have a solution at least from his end. The time it took for her to explain and the staff member to apologize and say that he cannot do anything worked in favour of the airline. The testing was completed and they announced that boarding has commenced for the flight. Even the lady who was very agitated with the treatment meted out to her had to quietly join the line and get onto the aircraft.

This scenario clearly shows how we are unable to clearly communicate our service expectations and that ends up being one of the key reasons for getting poor service.

If the passengers had focused on key service expectations, especially things which are doable, the situation might have been very different. For example, the passengers could have demanded refreshments which are very much within the control of the staff member at the boarding gate. Some of the passengers who were clear with regard to the expectation in terms of catching a connecting flight got their issue resolved. The other person who no longer wished to travel got a cancellation with refund. However, the majority who were waiting only got to hear about the experience of one passenger who had missed her flight.

This is the fundamental issue with getting poor service or not getting any service at all. As customers we do not know what to expect and more importantly when we do know, we do not communicate that expectation clearly.

Let me start by explaining the various service expectations a shopper has and how to get that service.

Basic and functional service is what happens in the majority of instances. This kind of service is largely about sharing basic information in a polite manner. In most cases, the information is template and the response of the service staff is standardized to the extent that it ends up sounding automated and therefore quite insincere. The best example for such a service is if you have called the customer helpline for any issue, the service staff would first say 'We are sorry and apologize for the inconvenience caused'. Unfortunately, such a template response has completely eradicated its value by making it patently insincere and therefore meaningless.

In some instances this basic and functional service actually becomes a disservice because of the way it is delivered. A scenario which most would have experienced is while parking, the security staff would, in many cases, watch you parking and when you would get out of the car, he would come over to say that you cannot park there. If the security guard had done this while, or ideally before, you had parked, it would have been appreciated.

This basic and functional service is the fundamental expectation of any shopper in any scenario. They want information pertaining to various things like product details, availability, etc. They expect this to be delivered in an efficient and polite manner. This is relatively easy to deliver and this is what shoppers tend to experience in mass merchandise stores like hypermarkets, etc. The staff members are there to give a basic level of information and assist in a minimal, functional way if required.

Even this basic, functional service starts to become complex in the context of certain product categories like consumer durables, electronics, mobiles, etc. This in turn calls for a higher level of training as well as a better quality of staff. For example, if a shopper was going to purchase soft drinks, their query might be limited to the location and asking about any promotional offer on the same. The same shopper might expect a higher level of information if they were to walk into a store to purchase an electric induction stove.

Responsive and personalized service is the next level of expectation in the minds of the shoppers. This kind of service requires the service staff to have a higher level of comprehension and understanding. This is required to understand the various dimensions of a shopper's enquiry. Let me explain this with an example.

An elderly gentleman once came to a consumer durables and electronics store and wanted to purchase the best laptop available. He was buying it for his daughter who had started her college education and had wanted a laptop. The staff members were very helpful and ended up selling a top-end laptop which was very expensive. The customer was back the very next day and was extremely angry. His daughter had wanted a basic laptop and when presented with the top-end one, she was happy but also puzzled. Her father then went on to highlight how she should now study very well, etc., as he was spending so much for her education. At that juncture she had to explain to him that he had purchased an expensive laptop whereas it was not required at all. A basic one would have cost one third the price paid by that gentleman.

This shopper was angry because he felt, and to some extent rightly so, that the staff had fooled him into buying an expensive laptop. The reality is that the service required by the gentleman was guidance regarding the purchase and a personalized solution. Instead, the store staff chose to provide a basic level of service by taking the words of the shopper at face value. The shopper had asked for the best available laptop and ended up being sold one, even though that was not the actual need or requirement.

Apart from understanding the shopper needs, responsive and personalized service also requires that the staff identify the broad kinds of shopper profiles and shopping behaviours. For example, in the anecdote above, if the shopper had been a Millennial, the response of the staff would have been perfectly fine because their shopping behaviour is very different.

Another scenario where responsive and personalized service tends to cross a line and ends up irritating the shopper is when the staff does not know when to back off and leave the shopper alone. I have experienced this often and I am sure that everyone has also had a similar experience of the store staff following them around all the time. Recently, I was browsing in a food store at the Bengaluru airport and looking at the varied range of snacks on display. Four different staff members came up to me and asked if I was looking for something specific. I had to politely decline their offer of help. One of the same staff members came back again to check if I required any help and that is when I left that store without purchasing anything. Ironically, this was not a large store and the few customers present and the staff were all quite visible to each other.

This is very annoying and actually might stop a potential shopper from making purchases because of the constant intrusions. However, if I had planned on buying something I would have firmly told the staff to leave me alone if they wanted me to purchase anything.

Relationship oriented service is when the store staff or the owner focuses more on establishing a rapport with the shopper. The owners of the small neighbourhood stores are masters at this and conversely the staff in the large, modern stores is not very good at doing this. The power of relationship-oriented service is very strong and ends up becoming a powerful element to create shopper loyalty.

An elderly lady would regularly come to the supermarket chain we had started in the '90s. Apart from her visits for shopping, she had a routine of dropping into the store every afternoon without fail. She would spend time browsing and also interacting with the various staff members. After spending quite a bit of time interacting with everyone, she would purchase a few things and leave. This used to happen like clockwork, every day.

I was quite intrigued and since I had observed her having long conversations with our customer service staff, asked them about her afternoon visits. I was quite surprised to know that she came into the store to talk and interact with the staff. Her children were all settled abroad and her husband had a habit of afternoon siesta. She did not like to sleep in the day and would be very bored in the afternoons. When the supermarket opened, it was like a boon to her as the staff members were smart and she could interact with them. What started off as an occasional visit to chat and interact with the store staff became a regular habit. She would come in every day in the afternoon for her chat session and also purchase a few items while leaving. This might seem odd and even funny but the reality is that this is what relationship-oriented service is all about. It is about interactions and that forms the basis of a relationship which leads to sales.

Another example in an online context for relationship-oriented service is that of an American online apparel and shoe retailer named Zappos. They are well known for their customer friendly policies and focus on customer service. Being an online retailer, they operate a large customer service call centre to cater to their various customers, many of whom are women. Incidentally, they also hold the record for the longest customer service call which is supposed to have lasted close to 10 hours on 10 December 2012 which broke the earlier record also held by Zappos, which was for approximately 9 hours.

The record-breaking customer service call was largely about the customer chatting about the experience of living in Las Vegas and incidentally also included the purchase of a pair of shoes. Other such long calls have been about personal issues, just wanting to talk, etc. This is not unlike the elderly lady who would come into the supermarket mainly to chat.

Interestingly enough, this service approach might not work for men who are very transactional in their shopping as discussed in an earlier chapter. This was reinforced during a workshop where I was discussing the role of service and what constitutes service with the participants. A particular chain of supermarkets was mentioned as an example for good service by a lady participant. All the men in the group immediately refuted this lady's statement claiming that the store was crowded and the staff did not know enough details about the products. In summary, the men were of the opinion that the store had very poor service. When the lady was quizzed about her perception as to why she felt that the same store had very good service, her response was typically influenced by her gender. She felt that the store offered very good service as the staff would talk to her, enquire about things and essentially deliver relationship-oriented service. The men in the group did not understand this as their expectations are largely about basic, functional service or responsive, personalized service in the case of few product categories.

In a similar manner the service expectations of a shopper would change based on their age as well as the product category being purchased. Gen X shoppers have different service expectations from Millennials and that would also differ based on what they are purchasing.

This complexity of service expectation is one of the main barriers as to why shoppers do not get good service. I am sure that a lot of what you have read till now is not known to you and might even appear to be contradictory and confusing, initially. It is only when all the pieces of the jigsaw puzzle fall into place that some amount of clarity will emerge about your shopping behaviour.

The typical store staff member in most retail outlets are high school pass outs, college dropouts or at best graduates. Their inputs consist largely of a few days of training wherein a large amount of information is shared with them and then they are sent to the store to work. It is near impossible for them to be able to comprehend all these multiple dimensions of providing service. This understanding might grow over years due to experiences and the related learning.

For example, in a sari shop the older salesman will always have a different and better way of managing his interactions with shoppers. He tailors his services and juggles between three types of service expectations depending on the shopper. It would be near impossible to teach all these and train a young, new salesperson.

Therefore, as shoppers we have three choices:

- Be oblivious to all these and one would end up having an equal chance of getting good or bad service.
- Be aware of all these factors but do nothing about it. Therefore, be thankful for good service and become tolerant of bad service.
- Be a smart shopper and manage the shopping interaction to maximize the probability of good service.

Let us examine how you can be a smart shopper in the context of service. However, before that, let me explain why we don't get good service. We don't get good service because no one has taught us how to go about it. Thus, what happens is that we behave in a manner which might elicit a positive response or not. Therefore, we become dependent on the customer service staff to provide good service.

Let me clarify before continuing that I am not at all absolving the store, delivery or call centre staff about their role and responsibility in providing service. My contention is that they are often constrained by their background, inexperience, and are unable to deliver the right kind of service. This tends to become good or bad depending on the shopper. My contention is that a smart shopper can get the right and appropriate service response in line with their expectations, which becomes good service as it meets their expectations.

In that context, the first constraint to getting good service is having the wrong expectation.

Waiting at the billing counter is by far the biggest irritant for any shopper. They might have spent hours inside the store browsing and shopping but even a few minutes of delay will put off the shopper and make them angry. A chain of stores realized this issue and came up with a plan to minimize, if not eliminate, the waiting period at the billing counter. They decided to use small handheld devices similar to smartphones and these would be used to bill the purchases for customers who did not have too many items. The retailer also advertised this facility stating that there will not be long billing queues henceforth.

However, this did not turn out the way it was planned mainly because the shopper expectations got defined in a very different way. They ignored the qualifier of 'long' in the advertisements and understood the message to mean that there will be no queues for billing. This is an impossible expectation in the Indian context where crowds are a part of everyone's daily life. This expectation made them indifferent to the efforts of the retailer in reducing the billing time through the use of handheld devices.

Shopper expectation, both in terms of setting the right ones and managing the same, is a huge challenge in delivering good service. Retailers who set the right expectation and meet the same gain credibility and trust. A case in point is regarding the delivery period mentioned in various online sites. As mentioned in an earlier chapter, shoppers tended to ignore the term 'business days' and would assume that the delivery would happen based on the number they saw. Several online retailers have realized this and that is why they mention an actual delivery date in order to set the right expectation. In reality this might actually mean the same thing. However, if a shopper gets the delivery on the date he expects, the trust level with that online retailer goes up.

Shopper expectations can also be unrealistic and sometimes illogical like what happened during the launch of a hypermarket store.

An elderly man came to the store a day after the launch and he was extremely upset and angry. He was cursing the customer service staff who had assisted him and wanted action to be taken against him. Upon enquiry, we found that he had come into the store and wanted to buy footwear for his grandson and gift it as a surprise. However, he did not know the exact size of the required footwear and was asking the staff member to guess the same based on the grandson's age and approximate height.

The expectation that the staff member would be able to accurately guess the size was completely irrational. It so happened that the size was wrong and the customer had come back to exchange the footwear. During this interaction he started to vent his frustration that he had not been able to surprise his grandson by blaming the customer service staff with not giving him the correct size.

Expectations can even be bizarre like the suggestion made by a shopper at a store in Hyderabad. This store had a liquor section which was quite popular. The store used to invite feedback and suggestion and a system was in place to interact with every shopper who gave any such feedback or suggestion. Imagine our surprise when one shopper sent in a suggestion that since there was a liquor section already in the store, we should open a small bar next to it. His rationale was that men could have a drink and relax while their family finished their shopping. In spite of a firm refusal to even consider this as a valid suggestion or feedback, he was quite persistent about the idea for a while.

A smart shopper would always do a reality check about whether his expectations are doable, practical and possible to fulfil.

While shopping for clothes during a festival we were handed out discount coupons which were valid for a minimum purchase value and could be availed only on the next purchase. This meant that the discount could not be applied on the same bill which entitled me to get these coupons. I had to come back again to get that benefit. However, I also noticed that the next purchase could be done at any time as there was no date or time restriction on the same.

I requested the person doing the billing to hold on and split my purchases into two bills. The first bill would entitle me to the discount coupons. The same coupons can then be used for getting the discount on the second bill. The cashier was not very enthusiastic about this request as the intention of the discount coupon was to make shoppers come to the store again for repeat purchase. My request clearly defeated that objective. I then requested for the supervisor to be called and repeated my request to him. I also added that since the coupon did not have any time or date restriction, my request was very much doable. Finally, they had to do what I requested of them and extend the discount on the second bill.

Suppose the coupons had a date or time restriction that said that the coupons would be valid only after a particular date or time, my expectation of getting the offer on the second bill would not be possible. In such a case, the supervisor might also have been powerless to do anything as their billing system would not have allowed the discount to be given for any shopper. That is the main reason why a smart shopper needs to have realistic expectations which can be fulfilled by the retailer.

Unrealistic expectations are usually handled by the store staff through polite smiles and repeatedly saying that it is not possible to cater to such an expectation. There are situations where the store staff try to avoid doing something even though the shopper's expectation is doable and can be met.

Take the same scenario of the discount coupon and imagine a situation where the supervisor and maybe even the store manager chose to take a tough stand and say that they cannot make two bills for my purchase and therefore the discount cannot be given on a second bill. The shopper essentially has only two options left. Leave the products and walk out of the store without purchasing anything or pay for the purchases and accept the discount coupons quietly.

A smart shopper would obviously choose the first option. The rationale is that any retail outlet which is not customer-oriented and shopper friendly does not deserve support from any shopper.

A smart shopper might even choose the second option if the products purchased are not available anywhere else, the prices are unbeatable, it is convenient or for any other reason which favours the shopper.

However, a lot of shoppers would react in an emotional manner and start an argument or a fight about this issue with the staff. Very soon the emotions would rule over the actual issue and both sides will end up taking a hard stand. As the emotions peak, the stands would harden to such an extent that no solution would then be possible.

This is somewhat similar to what happens in any incident of road rage. Any minor traffic infraction can be easily resolved if both parties choose to look at the issue and the resultant damage in an objective manner. However, that is rarely done. Instead, the common response would be to get off the bike or get out of the car and start the interaction with anger instead of objectivity.

Participants in, almost, every customer-service training are usually told that 'the customer is always right'. This statement is completely wrong and not possible at all. Customers or shoppers are human beings and can never be always right. In fact, in many instances, they are completely in the wrong. Yet, this mantra is told at every training programme and there is a reason for the same.

The rationale for making the service staff believe that the customer is always right is related to emotions. The customer feels and thinks that they are always right and that is driven by their emotions. It is not a rational or an objective thought. Therefore, the customer service staff are taught to approach any confrontation with the mindset that the customer is always right since that is what the customer is thinking. Most service guidelines would stress on first apologizing and calming the customer in any such situation. This is also aimed at addressing the emotional distress of the customer. This is a very important aspect of providing good service and establishing trust. Only after the customer has somewhat calmed down can any issue be resolved.

A case in point is the anecdote about the lady passenger who was angry because she had missed an earlier flight. The airline staff was not addressing her anger and frustration. This clearly led to a stalemate where her emotions continued to dominate her interaction. If the flight had been further delayed I am sure that the argument would have continued because she was actually voicing her emotions and not seeking a solution. If someone had asked her as to what she expected as a solution after she had calmed down, she might have been at a loss to explain. Retailers realize the importance of addressing the shopper's emotions and hence stress that 'The customer is always right'.

However, this is wrong as also not practically possible. Then, the question arises as to how one should handle a customer who is wrong but thinks that they are right. Let me share this anecdote to explain this better.

Lack of change is always a sensitive topic in any store. Smaller stores tend to give toffees in lieu of change if they don't have the right change. Larger stores try to avoid this practice as much as possible. In that context, retailers take a lot of effort to organize change. Apart from getting change from banks and the RBI, they even approach temples. The briefing to the cashiers in most stores is that they should be prudent in giving change to the shoppers. As such, most of them request the shopper for change if possible instead of handing out the change. This is largely because the majority of shoppers prefer to carry currency and pay by the same which results in a scenario that they need to be given change in return. The fact is that most of us tend to hand out currency notes of large denominations even for small value purchases. If one were to do a quick check at home, I am sure that most homes would have large quantities of change as we tend to keep these coins separately and invariably they are forgotten.

A regular shopper in one of the supermarket chains suddenly lost her temper one day when the cashier asked her if she had change. This was because the shopper gave a ₹500 note for a small purchase value. Being a regular shopper, the store manager knew her and went up to her, apologized and calmed her down. Once she had calmed down, the store manager explained about the various efforts taken to get change and also pointed out that shoppers keep handing out currency notes of large denomination for even a small bill value. Therefore, change was always in short supply and that is why the cashier had asked her for it.

Once her emotions had been addressed, the shopper understood the situation and left the store. Interestingly, she came back to the store to hand over some change. She said that she realized how much change keeps piling up at home and it would help the store as well as other shoppers if she gave it to the store.

This scenario became possible only because the manager addressed the shopper's emotional state first and helped her calm down. Imagine if the manager had said that the shopper was wrong and cannot become angry, what might have happened?

From a smart shopper's perspective the biggest barrier to get good service is the improper use of emotions. I am using the term improper because a shopper obviously is driven by the subconscious while shopping. Therefore, the whole activity is very obviously emotional in nature. The trick is to display the right emotion in the right measure and at the right time.

For example, a shopper who is unable to locate any customer service person for assistance needs to show some amount of anger briefly. This is required to get the desired assistance and service. However, if the same anger is continued to be shown, it might become counterproductive. In the same vein, shoppers should also be cautious about displaying keen interest and happiness, especially while bargaining. Let me share an anecdote to explain this point.

As mentioned before, male shoppers tend to be very functional by nature and that makes them very poor bargainers. During a business trip, I went shopping for a hand bag for my spouse. A lady colleague accompanied me as we had to go to an official event after the shopping was done. The desired hand bag had to conform to some exacting specifications in terms of compartments, etc. After checking a few small stores I found a bag which seemed to fulfil all the criteria and decided to purchase the same. The lady colleague had cautioned me that the quoted price in those shops was definitely up for bargaining and one could end up paying half or even less than that. Keeping that in mind, I asked for a ridiculously low price and the shop owner countered with a midway offer; he quoted a price between what he had originally asked for and what I offered. It seemed to be a good price and I got ready to pay when my lady colleague told the shop owner that the bag was not all that good and not worth the price he was asking for it. She went on to say how we would purchase the bag only if he reduced the price further as the bag itself was not exactly what we wanted.

I was surprised by her statement and instinctively turned to her and said that the bag was exactly what I was looking for and I wanted to purchase it. That display of emotion was enough for me to lose the negotiation with the shop owner. He calmly started to rearrange the display saying that he had already offered the best price. After having meekly paid the price and taken the bag, we stepped out and my colleague pointed out that we could have got a better price. She went on to explain how one should keep a totally disinterested expression while bargaining. Clearly this is an example of showing emotions inappropriately in a shopping scenario.

As a smart shopper, one should not only be clear about the expected outcome while seeking any service, but they should also express the right emotion, to the required extent. This tends to become a challenge as the emotional response of a person is often triggered by various aspects some of which are related to age, gender, cultural background, etc. However, if a shopper is able to manage all these and express the appropriate emotion, the service they get would always be above average, if not outstanding.

In the context of cultural influences, one of the major constraints why Indian shoppers tend to elicit poor service response is due to their approach to service. Indian, as well as several Asian, households tend to have servants even today. The very word servant is associated with a servile attitude. This refers to an attitude where the person displays an excessive willingness to serve or please others. It is a natural behavioural conditioning of any person who has grown up seeing servants being ordered around.

This conditioning and perception has been reinforced over the years by the kind of customer service staff we tend to see in our small neighbourhood stores. These stores employ helpers who are typically uneducated and from the village of the shop owner. Having come from rural as well as poor backgrounds, they often exhibit a servile attitude and don't mind if they are ordered around.

However, the scenario is changing in almost all service industries, especially in retail. The customer service staff one sees are at least high school pass outs, if not graduates. They are well-informed like most Millennials and have a higher level of self-esteem than the helper in a small neighbourhood store.

If shoppers behaved with customer service employees in the same manner in which they behave with their servants, the response would obviously not be very positive. In fact, the reality in most urban areas today is that no servant would tolerate rude behaviour and anyone ordering them around.

Nowadays, when engineering and management graduates are struggling for employment, service providers like maids, drivers, etc. are in great demand. Finding such people is difficult and they get employment in a relatively shorter time, especially if they are good at their jobs.

Smart shoppers should realize that service does not equal being servile. Customer service employees are not their servants to be ordered around. They are also engaged in a profession and need to be treated with courtesy and respect. This is exactly the issue that Indian passengers face with the staff of our national carrier. One can argue that this is not the case with private airlines and that would be completely wrong because of two elements.

The first reality is that passengers flying private airlines tend to display slightly, if not markedly, better behaviour. The second element is that even private airline staff responds to any rude behaviour and ordering around by ignoring the same as much as possible. In a worst-case scenario they escalate the matter and you would have read of instances where passengers were taken off the flight because of their behaviour.

Essentially service delivery is a two-way street and as shoppers we should put in efforts to be worthy of and deserving of good service.

In spite of all these, a shopper might still get bad service and that is largely due to poor communication. In my earlier book, I have written extensively about how a person can become a powerful communicator. Several stories, anecdotes and examples have been narrated to illustrate the stark difference in the outcome of any interaction if the person is a powerful communicator. There are 5 Cs which enable a person to become a powerful communicator. They are:

**Clarity:** The shopper should be clear about whether his expectations are appropriate and doable, or not.

**Conviction:** The shopper should have the conviction and confidence that they deserve what is being asked. Then, their communication also becomes powerful.

**Context:** The context of service expectation is very important. Any communication which is disproportionate with the context would never have any positive result.

**Customization:** This is an extremely crucial aspect. Shopper's communication should be customized and different for different people. One cannot communicate with a staff and the store manager in the same way.

**Communication:** Finally the actual communication, be it in person, over the phone or email, it is important that every aspect and detailing should be correct and appropriate.

You are welcome to read *Break Free* if you would like to know more about becoming a powerful communicator.

As a smart shopper, one needs to take ownership of getting good service. Although the customer service staff at any store, or an employee doing deliveries or the one at the call centre are responsible for delivering good service, smart shoppers should realize that they have an equal role to play.

## KEY TAKEAWAY

- Shoppers tend to be rude and demanding which puts off the service staff.
- Be clear about the service expectation and ensure that it is doable and practical.
- Customer or shopper cannot be right always.
- Emotions tend to colour the issue and influence the service level.
- Service does not mean servile and customer service staff members are not one's servants.
- Powerful communication is crucial to share expectations and thereby influences service levels.

## SMART SHOPPING HABITS

- Be clear of what to expect and ensure that it is relevant to the context.
- Control your emotions and leverage them to get good service.
- Ask for things which are possible and doable.
- Smart shoppers will always treat others with respect and not order anyone around.
- Always keep in mind that you have an equal role to play in getting good service.

# 9
# BECOMING A SMART SHOPPER

Shopping today is exciting, interesting and, also, so very confusing. There is a multiplicity of shopping options, products, and brands within various product categories. Making the right choice is not easy and that remains one of the key expectations for any shopper.

Comparatively, the older generation of shoppers actually had an easier time shopping simply because the extent of options and choices were limited. Their mindset was influenced by scarcity which made them focus on functional shopping. The choices available to them were also easy and simple.

The next generation of shoppers, the Gen Xers, started to experience more complexity in shopping with the advent of self-service stores. They could no longer pass on the shopping burden to the shop owner. The choices they made were their own and it started to redefine the way they shopped. Suddenly they were exposed to impulse buying and used to spend more without even being aware that they had purchased more.

During the early days of modern self-service stores, we conducted several shopper studies to understand their behaviour and perception. During one such study, the women in the focus group were all quite vociferous about how the new supermarket we had opened was expensive and making them spend more. Interestingly, they wanted to shop at this supermarket because of their children preferring to come to such stores instead of the small neighbourhood store. Pester power had started to make its presence felt from then onwards.

These ladies went on to say that even if the children had not insisted, they would still prefer the supermarkets for the shopping experience and the family time it helped to create. Explaining the family time perspective, they said that their spouse and children were ready to come for shopping at the supermarket and would not do so if it was the neighbourhood store. Over a period of time this behaviour has extended to malls, combining the functionality of shopping with an experiential aspect.

However, this preference was tempered by the fact that they were spending more in the supermarket which created a perception of it being expensive. The comment about supermarkets being expensive was of concern and the ladies were quizzed about the prices that they would normally pay for the key grocery items (KVI products explained in chapter 3) which formed the bulk of their monthly shopping. They were then asked to compare that with the prices they had paid at the supermarket. These women were quite surprised to see that the prices were actually lower. However, that did not convince them as their stand was that they ended up spending more at the supermarket as compared to the neighbourhood store.

The next step was to compare the list of items they used to purchase and what had been purchased at the supermarket. The ladies were shocked to discover that everyone had purchased more number of products at the supermarket and a few had purchased as much as 30 per cent more. This was clearly influenced by impulse shopping and that is possibly one of the biggest shifts in shopping behaviour that Gen X shoppers experienced in India with regard to online shopping.

Self-service formats and more recently online shopping has redefined the way shoppers behave. I can safely say that the Gen X shoppers have had to manage more changes to their shopping orientation and behaviour than any other generation including the Millennials.

Choice always creates challenges in any scenario. Similar is the case with shopping. One key fall-out of any choice is the doubt about whether the right choice was made. Many a times this leads to regret about the choices made. The example for this doubt is when you order a dish in a restaurant and after it has been served, the dish at the neighbouring table suddenly looks more appetizing.

There is even a term in consumer behaviour for this doubt and it is referred to as 'Buyer's Remorse' or 'Post-Purchase Dissonance'. Although, this regret and anxiety about having made the wrong choice is obvious in the case of large, high value purchases; it does exist in smaller doses for certain other product categories also.

The reason for buyer's remorse is actually simple in most cases. Shopping tends to be largely influenced by subconscious impulses and a person's rational thought is always slower to catch up with the same. Shoppers react based on this impulse at first and then question the same when their rational thought kicks in.

A related theory was espoused by an American psychologist Barry Schwartz in a book titled *The Paradox of Choices: Why More is Less*, published in 2004. In the book, he explains why multiplicity of choices after a particular level is not good as it does create anxiety and psychological distress.

However, the fact remains that we live in a world of multiple choices especially with regard to shopping. This does tend to complicate life and one way to manage this is to move towards a simpler life of functional purchases. That option is clearly not practically possible because of various aspects explained in the introduction, and mainly the availability of higher levels of disposable income with shoppers.

Higher disposable income with increased exposure to information drives the desire for better lifestyle which is what fuels shopping and retail. Therefore, the manufacturers will continue to offer more products and brands and retail options will only increase as time passes.

The alternative to simplistic, functional purchases is to aim at becoming a smart shopper. This is the objective of this book and all the various details and inputs shared in the earlier chapters. The aspects discussed in the book would help a shopper manage their behaviour better and make more informed purchase decisions. This would also help in reducing, if not eliminating, buyer's remorse and any related anxiety. More importantly, this change in shopping behaviour might be possible even in a scenario of complex and multiple choices.

However, the journey to becoming a smart shopper is not going to be easy or an instant one. This will take time and effort mainly because shopping is a habit and a deeply ingrained one at that.

Habit is a repetitive behaviour which might even be compulsive and in many cases your rational mind is unable to explain or rationalize this behaviour or activity. This repetitive behaviour could be because of any kind of influence starting from the beliefs and value systems that have been imbibed by you during childhood. Next is the impact of your peers, the cultural aspect as well as your personality, which influences such repetitive behaviour.

Although various influences might initiate an activity or behaviour, repetition is required for that to become a habit. Repetition would happen only if the experience is positive.

If the experience of that activity or behaviour is negative, repetition would not happen and therefore it will not become a habit. In consumer behaviour, they use the term 'learning' which refers to repetitive reinforcement. This learning defines whether something will become a habit or not. In many cases this learning can happen indirectly also through the experience of others.

The only way shopping behaviour can change is through conscious practice and the resultant learning. This would redefine the shopping behaviour. Shoppers who practice some of the smart shopper habits consciously would see a change in the way they shop and that would be a good start. However, repetitive reinforcement is required to turn these conscious actions into a habit. This calls for a higher level of awareness of how you shop and where you need to make changes.

The first step in the journey to becoming a smart shopper is to increase your awareness level with regard to your subconscious impulses. Second would be to allow some time for your rational thoughts to kick in. Shopping with a list helps a person do both these things. While following the list of items to be purchased you should question the impulse to pick up something which was not on the list. I have found a simple trick helps in doing this.

Put the product back on the shelf or do not click on the buy now button. Add that product to the end of your list and continue with your shopping. While you are going through the list, you mind would be mulling over the product you left behind. By the time you have finished picking up everything else, the impulse would have won or your rational thought would have convinced you that the product is not needed. You can then choose to forget it and leave; or go back to click on the buy button or pick up that product for purchase.

Either way, this practice would give your rational mind to play a part in the shopping decision and might also help manage buyer's remorse.

Shopping is a habit built largely on trust. This trust tends to blind most shoppers to certain aspects of their purchases. Over a period of time the shoppers tend to fall back on the habit instead of checking the various details while shopping. A simple example is with regard to the expiry dates on various products, especially food items. Most shoppers I have seen pick up products without checking even the basic details such as manufacturing date and expiry date. Ironically I have also seen shoppers indulge in behaviour which has no logic. For example I have seen shoppers pick up the second product as they believe that the first one must have been handled by other shoppers. The funny part of such behaviour is that the majority of shoppers end up picking up the second product because they all think in a similar manner.

Being aware and informed is helpful not only to control impulsive shopping but also to ensure that basic aspects pertaining to shopping are checked to avoid any surprises.

I can only hope that in my quest to share inputs to help you become a smart shopper, I have not taken the fun out of your shopping. That should definitely not happen and you should enjoy your shopping but with a higher level of awareness and prudence.

Try and follow the various smart shopper habits mentioned in the book and continue to enjoy your shopping experience. This is one of the indulgences that anyone can allow themselves and should definitely not be denied.

Last but not the least, I reiterate what was mentioned in the introduction. I am fairly confident that in spite of reading the book and understanding the various points there is a very high probability that you will still continue to be influenced more by your emotional, unconscious, impulsive decisions instead of the rational thought process.

Regardless of the level and extent to which you are able to practice the smart shopper habits and become a smart shopper yourself, it would help others if you shared your experiences in doing so. You can post your experiences on my Facebook page titled 'SMART Shopping' (search for @SMARTShoppingbook) as well as read about the experiences shared by other smart shoppers. The page would also be updated with other shopping-related news and inputs which might be of additional use to you as a smart shopper.

Scan this QR code to open
the
**SMART Shopping**
Facebook page.

# APPENDIX I

## KEY TAKEAWAY FROM EACH CHAPTER

## CHAPTER 1

- Shopping behaviour varies based on gender, age and the category of product being purchased.
- Men are more functional in their shopping approach while women might actually be better shoppers.
- Women might shop for a longer period but also finish more chores during that time.
- The older generation and Gen X are more functional and value driven.
- Millennials' priority while shopping is about latest trends and new features.

## CHAPTER 2

- Trust is the single most important element which defines shopping decisions.
- Shoppers tend to develop trust based on their experiences.
- The experiences must match or exceed the expectations in shoppers' minds for trust to be built.
- Shoppers make purchases based on perception which might not be correct. However, for them, their perception is the reality.
- Perception and trust often make the shoppers overlook or ignore key terms and conditions.

## CHAPTER 3

- There is no universally correct, right price.
- Price is not the same as value. Price is only a small element

which makes up the perception of value in a shopper's mind.
- Shoppers seek value and often mistake low prices for great value. This is incorrect.
- During the sale season, it is not worth going around comparing prices as the exact same products/models are rarely on sale.

## CHAPTER 4

- The five sensory influences trigger powerful responses as they impact the subconscious.
- Colours affect us physiologically as well as create strong imageries.
- Visual impact is leveraged through display of products that encourages purchase.
- Smell is the most powerful emotionally linked sense because it automatically triggers subconscious memories associated with a particular smell.
- Shoppers prefer self-service stores as they enable the 'Touch, Feel and See' experience. This is one of the key factors that drives impulse buying.

## CHAPTER 5

- Promotions leverage the universal reality that everyone likes to get something for nothing.
- Any free offer would only be attractive if it is relevant to the purchase. In the shopper's mind, the free product has value and utility.

- The most attractive and also the simplest promotion is always a straightforward discount.
- Promotions always leverage one or more of these feelings—sense of urgency, feeling of being special, and being able to make smart choices.

## CHAPTER 6

- Pester power is the influence children have on their parents' shopping behaviour.
- Retailers are aware of pester power and try to counter the same or leverage its power.
- The inputs of Millennials and the younger generation of shoppers play a big role in the shopping decisions of few product categories.
- Children are oblivious to the reaction of strangers which gives them the freedom to behave in whichever way they want. Parents are often not firm enough because they are concerned about what others would think.

## CHAPTER 7

- Online shopping is here to stay. However, physical stores are also not going anywhere.
- Convenience is the key trigger for online shopping. Subsequent factors like range of products and discounts are added attractions for shoppers.
- Online shopping fulfils the Millennial shopper's expectations of convenience, instant gratification, and availability of latest and trendy products.

- Gen X shoppers are also slowly warming up to online shopping because of the convenience factor as well as the fact that they have started to trust this shopping option.
- Shoppers are increasingly sharing information and data about themselves and their shopping behaviour in an extensive manner.
- BAFARA is a key shopper expectation which is what Omni Channel is trying to cater to.
- Technology will influence shopping and shopper-behaviour to a large extent in the coming years.
- Virtual Reality and Mixed Reality might soon bring the store to your home.

## CHAPTER 8

- Shoppers tend to be rude and demanding which puts off the service staff.
- Be clear about the service expectation and ensure that it is doable and practical.
- Customer or shopper cannot be right always.
- Emotions tend to colour the issue and influence the service level.
- Service does not mean servile and customer service staff members are not one's servants.
- Powerful communication is crucial to share expectations and thereby influences service levels.

# APPENDIX II

## SMART SHOPPING HABITS

## CHAPTER 1

- Men should always shop with a list. Chances of missing out things would be less.
- Women can verbalize the to-do list in their minds when shopping with a male as this would avoid misunderstandings.
- When shopping for a woman, focus on the sensory aspect and appeal. The reverse should be done when shopping for men; focus more on the functional and utility aspects in that case.
- When shopping with or for Millennials, focus on the latest, trendy categories. Millennials who are shopping for their parents should keep in mind that their parents have a different orientation and might not appreciate the same thing.
- Avoid being judgemental about different shopping orientations. Each is an outcome of certain influences and has its own advantages.

## CHAPTER 2

- Develop a questioning mindset with regard to shopping. Don't accept anything at face value.
- Be well informed about the products you purchase. This will minimize the dependence on the shop owner or staff.
- Pay attention to the terms and conditions and other details while shopping. Trust should not make you assume things.

## CHAPTER 3

- Remember that there is no universal right price. Price is relative to the expectation of quality.
- Research and get information as well as details about the products to be purchased. This would help in determining the correct price point.
- Use the Internet and smartphones for searching. However, be prudent in trusting whatever you see online.
- Be aware of your preferred price point and try to stick to the same.
- Male shoppers should learn to bargain in order to become smart shoppers.

## CHAPTER 4

- Be aware of the impact of these sensory elements.
- Curb the tendency to react impulsively to any of these sensory influences.
- Allow the rational mind to process the information and help you take a logical decision.
- If you wish to limit your shopping, consciously avoid touching the products on display.
- Exercise before shopping; it would tire you as well as increase your Dopamine levels.
- Eat before shopping, preferably ripe bananas.
- If you feel the need to indulge in some retail therapy, stick to window shopping at those stores which are not open.

## CHAPTER 5

- Practice becoming aware of which feeling is getting triggered: urgency, feeling special or being smart.
- Consciously focus on some rational thinking when feeling any impulse or emotional response towards promotional offers.
- Check all the details of any product on promotion, especially the expiry date.
- Eat before going to a sale. Eating makes you feel satiated and you would be less likely to feel the scarcity urge.
- Shop with a list and try to stick to it. This would help you focus and shift your attention away from promotional offers.

## CHAPTER 6

- Take children along for product categories which might not be of interest to them and therefore they will curtail your shopping.
- Cultivate the habit of smart shopping in children by making them take ownership and responsibility with regard to money.
- Involve them in shopping by giving them a list and make them shop for those items.
- Give them some amount of money to purchase what they wish while shopping. This amount should not be increased without any valid reason.
- Never feel awkward about disciplining children who are not behaving properly while shopping.

## CHAPTER 7

- Be aware and careful about the extent of information being shared online.
- Try to shop online using the computer instead of the app, and log in and log out every time. Every additional activity or work you do will help to manage impulsive shopping.
- Avoid saving and storing your credit card details on any online shopping site.
- Have a separate credit card with a lower credit limit.
- Clear the cookies and the cache on your computer and smartphone regularly.

## CHAPTER 8

- Be clear of what to expect and ensure that it is relevant to the context.
- Control your emotions and leverage them to get good service.
- Ask for things which are possible and doable.
- Smart shoppers will always treat others with respect and not order anyone around.
- Always keep in mind that you have an equal role to play in getting good service.

# ACKNOWLEDGEMENTS

Thanks to Dr Saundarya Rajesh, my spouse, whose shopping behaviour was amongst the first I got to observe. The learning from it started much later as I became a retailer. Her constant motivation to encourage me to share what I know is one of main reasons behind this book.

Thanks to my children, Akshey and Shivangi, the Millennials. Their perspective on shopping, especially online shopping, has given me great insights.

Thanks to all my retail colleagues who would share their observations and discuss shopping-behaviour and its various perspectives.

Thanks to all my students as well as the participants of my training programmes with whom I would discuss and debate about shopping behaviour. Their questions, observations and the sharing of their own experiences have added to my learning.

This book was actually conceived by me in 2011–12 and Mr Kapish Mehra was very supportive of the idea. Finally it has become a reality in 2017. Thanks to Mr Mehra for his support in making this book a reality and Ms Amrita Mukherji who championed this book idea the second time around.

Thanks to the editorial team at Rupa Publications, especially Shambhu Sahu, who helped in ironing out the wrinkles and making this book better. There are so many others at Rupa

Publications who have worked behind the scenes for this book and my sincere gratitude to all of them in the designing, production, sales and marketing teams.

How could I forget Master Shifu, our beloved pug? He is my constant companion as I write and also my main source of distraction. I am sure that if he could shop, a whole new dimension of shopper-behaviour would unfold.